Praise for Lessons from t

"In *Lessons from the Empress*, authors Cassandra Snow and Siri Plouff have offered a unique and deep exploration of the tarot using the archetype of The Empress as your guide in your journey toward self-care and creative growth. As you move through the workbook, you'll find magical rituals, suggestions for self-care, unique tarot spreads, and generous creative prompts, all woven together beautifully to support and nurture your spirit. The message here: be indulgent, make art, and let magic enter every area of your life! This is the book we all need in today's turbulent times."

—Theresa Reed, author of *Twist Your Fate: Manifest Success with Astrology and Tarot*

"In *Lessons from the Empress,* Snow and Plouff go beyond the Empress's superficial social media meme to show that embracing the archetype isn't just about crystals and bubble baths. It's an act of digging deep into your soul to find your authentic, creative, and bountiful self."

—Rashunda Tramble, coauthor of *The Numinous Tarot Guide: A New Way to Read the Cards*

"In *Lessons from the Empress*, Snow and Plouff have combined their considerable wealth of knowledge to share powerful and useful tips on integrating creativity into daily life through the use of tarot cards. From reminding us that creativity is our birthright to providing a self-care equation tying in all four suits of the deck, this book is packed with personal stories, original tarot spreads, and helpful insights on using the cards for inspiration, expression, and discovery. *Lessons from the Empress* is an excellent resource for anyone looking for inclusive, accessible methods for integrating tarot into their creative workings."

—Meg Jones Wall, author of *Finding the Fool: A Tarot Journey for Radical Transformation*

"*Lessons from the Empress* brings tarot to life! With a pack of cards in hand, you'll find this is your guidebook to better mental and spiritual wellness. When the world needs these lessons the most, Snow and Plouff come through for us all."

—Benebell Wen, author of *Holistic Tarot*

LESSONS
from the
EMPRESS

LESSONS
from the
EMPRESS

A TAROT WORKBOOK
for Self-Care
and Creative Growth

Cassandra Snow *and* **Siri Vincent Plouff**

foreword by Lisa Marie Basile

WEISER
BOOKS

This edition first published in 2022 by Weiser Books, an imprint of
Red Wheel/Weiser, LLC
With offices at:
65 Parker Street, Suite 7
Newburyport, MA 01950
www.redwheelweiser.com

ISBN: 978-1-57863-793-5
Library of Congress Cataloging-in-Publication Data available upon request.

Cover and text design by Sky Peck Design
Interior images used by permission: The Empress and The Fool from
The Radiant Tarot © Alexandra Eldridge, 2021; The Nurturer from *The Numinous Tarot* © Cedar
McCloud, 2018; The Empress from *The Shining Tribe Tarot* © Rachel Pollack, 2001.

Typeset in Arno Pro

Printed in the United States of America
IBI
10 9 8 7 6 5 4 3 2 1

*This book is dedicated to the memory of the incomparable Jane Hawkner,
luminary and friend in life and death.*

"*The artist seeks contact with his intuitive sense of the gods, but in order to create his work, he cannot stay in this seductive and incorporeal realm. It's the artist's responsibility to balance mystical communication and the labor of creation.*"

—PATTI SMITH, *Just Kids*

CONTENTS

PART ONE

PREPARING THE WAY FOR THE EMPRESS

PART TWO

THE MAJOR ARCANA: THE INWARD JOURNEY

PART THREE

THE MINOR ARCANA: THE JOURNEY TO SELF-ACCEPTANCE

FOREWORD

As children, creativity was our universal language. Do you remember? We spoke it fluently, and with ease. In fact, we only need to think back on our childhoods to know that creativity is a natural state, emanating from within.

We'd wake on a Sunday morning, stretch our limbs, and tumble into the dewy grass or build a castle of sand. We created because it felt good and right, and because it helped us care for ourselves. It helped us grow. Even as children, we *knew* this. We *knew* that joy and purpose were something worth creating. We were tiny spell-casters, and our words were our wands. Our imaginations were incantations.

It didn't matter if we wrote little "books" of poetry (the pages haphazardly stapled together), told stories to our invisible friends, or envisioned a quest through the stars as we peered out the window into the evening sky. We could easily create these whole worlds and fall headfirst into them. We changed our reality by daydreaming, by drawing, by writing, by dancing, by storytelling.

This, I believe, is where magic comes from: the mysterious but oh-so-real impulse to make life more beautiful, more joyful, and to feel connected. It is inherently within us and as luscious as flowers or silk—but that magic becomes stagnant and quiet if we don't tend to it. This is how The Empress can nurture us. The Empress tells us to take stock of our senses, to express ourselves wholly and truly, and to access the Venusian because we deserve it.

Sadly, The Empress's energy is often dismissed. We are pushed to ignore or forget its ways, especially in today's capitalist trenches. Especially when we are marginalized and fighting for safety and inclusion. Especially when we are told we are not good enough or talented enough or beautiful enough to dress in proverbial satin or sleep in the proverbial meadow of our imaginations.

The world tells us to live in false binaries and clean lines, to be rational, to not "waste" time on creativity without purpose. That art and pleasure and magic are relics of another time or are reserved for only certain people.

But we know better. This is why you're here—reading this book. And this is why I am writing this, right now. Because The Empress tells us to make space for flowers, for light, for growth, for what's in between the lines, for messages from beyond what we see before us: to close our eyes and describe what we feel, to light a candle and divine an image within its dancing flame, to allow the Major Arcana to unfold the worlds we hold within us, to let the archetypes pull us into a garden of reflection and lessons and growth. Because life is deeper and more lush when we understand our Towers and our Stars.

"The Empress teaches us that acts of creation are the ultimate practice of self-care. This authentic self, this abundant space, is not something we go find—it's something we *create*," Plouff and Snow write.

And, as Plouff and Snow express, creativity isn't hinged on any one definition. No, the creative self is the self that creates and indulges for the *sake* of creation and pleasure: dance, baking, arranging aromatic flowers, penning poems to read only to the moon, or creating a soft and nurturing home. It's about casting a circle and saying, "I am here." Their book reminds us of this— this abundance of "peak-season flowers and freshly baked bread," as they write—because it's our birthright.

This book is a safe and affirming playground, a space where creative inspiration is on tap. It is the altar and the devotion itself. It is a space of color and texture and truth and magic—a magical medicine. And as a poet-witch, I find myself inspired with each turn of the page, with each exploration of any given tarot card.

To create truly is to make something from nothing—a sort of divinity. This is why I believe poems are spells and rituals are doorways to a new life.

To turn over a tarot card is to open the door and walk through. What is the lesson or the message? What is an act of creativity that can help bring you closer to yourself? What might the cards inspire? How will this help you access self-care? In a world of chaos and sorrow, your tarot deck and your notebook can provide an anchor point.

What Plouff and Snow have done in this book is forged a candlelit pathway—accessible and encouraging, inclusive and actionable—that you can call your own. It balances instruction with reader autonomy. Its beauty is found in its absolute devotion to the creative spirit, welcoming interpretation and self-dialogue, and creating confidence through your journey.

Lessons from the Empress calls to the part of us that we are so often told to shut off and tidy up and suppress. It asks us to pick up the Wand and arrange a bed of flowers. It asks us to lift our Cup and breathe in the color and speak in music. It asks us to befriend the Swords and tell your deepest story. It asks us to connect with the Pentacles, our hands covered in wet soil as we reflect on what abundance truly means.

Are you ready to walk into the rose garden?

Are you ready to create the rose garden itself?

Pull a card. Start the journey.

—LISA MARIE BASILE,
author of *The Magical Writing Grimoire*

INTRODUCTION

When you conjure up an image of the tarot's Empress card, what do you see? In my mind, The Empress is seated on a throne in a lush and verdant landscape, wearing a luxuriant robe and holding a shield with the symbol for Venus on it. The Empress is at ease with themself, well taken care of and satisfied—not only satisfied with the surrounding abundance but also satisfied because The Empress has created things: this robe, this shield, this garden, even this throne. Everything around The Empress began as an idea—a seed—and they got busy planting, creating, and nurturing every last seed into being. This is how we see The Empress represented in the Rider-Waite-Smith Tarot deck and, even though the tarot is being constantly reimagined and updated, this take on The Empress endures, consistently rendered in a way that captures the ideal Venusian Creatrix.

As a set of seventy-eight cards, the tarot has endless lessons to teach us. Creative types and marginalized people are often distinctly drawn to the lessons of The Empress. The Empress has learned to collaborate with the land and create a nurturing space of abundance and peace. The Empress is free to be completely themself in this creation that they birthed into existence—made both *from* them and *for* them. This is what all of us are always trying to do—create our most authentic selves into being and hold space for them in a place of abundance and peace. The Empress teaches us that acts of creation are the ultimate practice of self-care. This authentic self, this abundant space, is not something we go find—it's something we *create*.

Lessons from the Empress is a labor of love to the tarot itself and to the community of creators who want to use it to amplify and deepen their work via the tarot. This is not necessarily a book for professional tarotists or artists, though they will certainly find plenty in these pages. This is a book for anyone who is anywhere on a tarot or creative journey, who wants a unique viewpoint or an unseen way to dig deeper. In particular, this is a book for those who feel marginalized. Almost every artist we know is marginalized in some way, and almost every marginalized person we know creates in some way. We want to show that creativity is a vital piece of self-care, and that self-care is necessary for anyone fighting the good fight day in and day out. Then we want to show you how the tarot can take you deeper and make you prouder of your voice and your work than you ever dreamed possible.

Our goal with *Lessons from the Empress* is to give you the tools you need to do just that. We believe that working toward The Empress's ideals of nurturance via self-care—to the point of luxury, self-expression, and creation—are vital to a holistic, satisfying life. The tarot has all the information you need to embrace these ideals yourself. The Empress has an abundance of lessons to teach you, ways to love, support, and speak for yourself. You just have to walk through the journey to internalize them.

Getting to Know the Empress

The Empress is the third card of the Major Arcana. Common interpretations of The Empress include abundance, indulgence, and creation. We see the figure on the card as one deeply involved with growth and self-care. The images on page xvii show many different ways The Empress energy is internalized and depicted by various artists. While the keyword of "creation" is traditionally seen through the eyes of motherhood, modern tarot readers are moving our understanding of creation more expansively toward joy and self-care via self-expression and creativity. The Empress teaches us to tend to

Depictions of The Empress: top row: *The Rider Tarot* and *The Radiant Tarot*; bottom row: *The Numinous Tarot* and *The Shining Tribe Tarot*. Used by permission.

ourselves. When we do so, our self-expression blooms. We create ourselves. The Empress has come to be the significator for artists and a sigh of relief in a reading about creativity. The abundance The Empress speaks of is different from what we see in, say, the Nine of Pentacles (also a card of abundance). Through The Empress we are connected more deeply to our physical senses of taste, sight, smell, hearing, and touch. This abundance calls to mind the feeling of something truly delightful to take in, something dancing just for you within your line of sight. This is the abundance of the fragrances of peak-season flowers and freshly baked bread, the kind of abundance you sink into, enjoying the luxury of incomparably soft sheets beneath you.

Yes, the abundance of The Empress differs from the simply material abundance of the Nine of Pentacles. Empress abundance is one of comfort. It is knowing that through self-expression, self-nurturance, and self-care you have created a wealth of art, joy, and support. The Empress is every bit as connected to materia and nature as that earth element Nine of Pentacles. Yet here, instead of thinking about what we have created with the given materia, we are working easily *in partnership* with the materia. This is the abundance of collaboration with the world itself, the gardens we grow, the art journals we design carefully, the words used to pinpoint the perfect scene in our fan fiction. It is an abundance that fills us not just with pride, but also with gratitude, connection, and love for all of the things we're working with.

The entire Major Arcana is meant to speak to us spiritually in big, deep, personal ways, and what is more personal than the things we create? In the modern day, "creativity" is often misinterpreted as something professional artists, wannabe artists, and kids engage in. Beyond that, if you've opted not to make it your life, you've opted out of it. Yet the tarot makes it clear that it is an innate part of us—we are creative beings. More importantly, it is a deeply divine part of us. In my own life, I've seen art kick-start important conversations and jump-start someone's activism. I've seen it raise awareness of important issues. In 2017, *TheWrap* published an article about *Will and Grace*'s effect on the push for marriage equality, and that is just one example of the many ways that popular culture brings a creativity that impacts our lives.

I want to specifically point out that seeing lesbians, non-binary, fat, and disabled people in art has always had an enormous impact on me. My own coming out to myself was the result of seeing "lipstick lesbian" Genesis on MTV's The Real World: Boston and realizing that being exactly who I am was possible. The catchphrase is that "representation matters," but recent conversations in the public forums of Twitter, Instagram, and TikTok posit that that phrase doesn't go far enough. The push for #ownvoices in publishing and media is critical. This very book is in this spirit and lineage. We've seen how the world changes by mere representation. Finding existing creative work that reflects who we are, using that to root and thrive as our very selves—these are beautiful, Empress acts of self-care. Imagine how powerful that change can be when people are actively giving space to queer, BIPOC, and disabled creators.

As the next step on our self-care journey, we can recognize that creativity is not just for the chosen few but that it is our own birthright to create. In fact, creativity as the ultimate form of self-care is self-expression exalted. Self-care is a buzzword for a reason right now. It is *important* to take care of ourselves via boring self-care acts like brushing our teeth and taking our meds *and* via the more Empress-like forms that make us feel powerful and abundant. This might include bubble baths and champagne, buying a whole cake rather than just a slice, or filling your home with plants and offbeat decor. For me it's all of those things, rotated around so it always feels like a treat. The Empress unequivocally speaks to the importance of self-care. "Nurturance" as a keyword absolutely means nurturance and care of self in modern day. This card invokes that part of us driven not only to survive but also to thrive. For that, we absolutely, beyond a shadow of a doubt, need self-care.

To fully practice self-care, we need to know what it is that we want and need. That knowing will come from internal self-expression: you having that conversation with yourself and coming to an awareness of your desires. Then we need to express those desires to others, so we are able to carve out the space and acquire the time and resources we need for self-care. Creativity itself, art itself—so much of it comes down to self-expression. All of what is created in the world at large, all of that came because of someone's decision to express what was on their mind or in their heart.

The Empress honors that part of us that has Things. To. Say. They honor that part of us that strives to create but doesn't know where to start. They honor that part of ourselves that wants to engage and indulge all parts of our being. This is especially true for those who have been hurt, cast aside, or traumatized. To truly come into our own and embody The Empress, we must learn to listen to their lesson—and there are some additional steps we don't want to skip. That's where ritual, the rest of the tarot, and *practice* come in.

We use ritual and magic in this book as additional tools to help you get in touch with your inner Empress. At the end of each card section, you will find prompts for self-care, prompts for self-expression, rituals, and spells specific to the tarot, and a selection of tarot spreads to work with the Major Arcana and each suit in the Minor Arcana. In this book, we are weaving together a variety of different ideas to show how ritual, magic, and tarot are connected and we encourage you to see them all as manageable. Noted Renaissance-era alchemist, astrologer, and occultist John Dee was also a brilliant stagehand who still remains largely unmatched in creating practical effects for theatre. Also worth noting here is Pamela Colman Smith, who also worked in the theatre as both set and costume designer: Smith's art brought the modern tarot to life. There's a reason for that: ritual and creativity go hand in hand. These ideas are deeply embedded into your tarot deck. Working with both tarot and magic in this way, we become exalted and transformed into someone not unlike The Empress. That is to say, someone not afraid to be indulgent, capable of brilliant creation, and able to prioritize what's best for us. Ritual and magic unlock the door to self-care. Tarot takes you on the journey.

Ritual and magic are inherently creative. You are *writing* spells, *baking* bread, *designing* sigils. Through magic and ritual you are trying to *create* an outcome or a change. Just as we believe everyone is psychic, everyone can think logically, everyone can tune in to their body in a non-harmful way, we also believe that every single one of us is creative. It is our birthright to indulge that deeply embedded desire to make things. Ritual is one way that this can be unlocked and centered.

Tarot is much more creative than people give it credit for, both as a container for occultist thought (just ask the spirits of Lady Frieda Harris, who did the art for the *Thoth Tarot* or Pamela Colman Smith) and as a modern tool that pushes us to think outside the box. Thinking outside the box is literally creative thinking; it is the first spark of bringing back The Empress inside all of us. While we may back-burner the desire to create when it isn't making money (and some of us attempt to kill it off altogether), our creativity never dies. We can always tap back into it when we're ready. Tarot is one of the best ways to show us how, and this workbook should deepen your tarot understanding, your ability to speak for and care for yourself, and unleash all of that beautiful creativity swirling around inside of you. In other words, this book should help you take in and express all of The Empress's beautiful lessons.

Take the prompts, ideas, and activities we've written in this book and create space in your life to explore them more fully. Maybe you'll end up with new insight into the Divine, yourself, or the world. Maybe you'll end up with a cool project or a handful of small projects that the world has never seen before. Maybe you'll unlock this side of yourself permanently, and maybe you just need a single catharsis to let some old stuff go. In any case, there will be a synthesis and *you* will have created something. That is beautiful, and brilliant, and it is why we are here.

The Empress is ready to open up and teach us valuable lessons to kick-start our journey of self-care and creative expression. So let's get started with some basics.

· ·

Pull out your journal (or at least your thinking cap) and start finding answers to these questions:

1. What does self-care mean and look like to you now? When do you do self-care? What type of self-care do you do? How much of it is magical?

How much of it is related to art, media, or creativity? Is it a sustaining practice or "as needed"?

2. What does self-expression mean to you now? Do you make time and save energy to express yourself? What might shifting that way or incorporating more room for it look like for you?

3. Jot down a few ideas about what creativity means to you before moving on. When you hear a phrase like "unlock your creativity" or "engage your creative spirit," what springs to mind? Put another way, what do you create? Your ideas are *not* wrong, even if they don't match ours—really let yourself run loose here.

4. What are some goals that you have for self-care and self-love? What does embodying The Empress look like for you, personally? We have lots of ideas in this book, but this is *your* journey! Self-expression, self-care—they contain and lead with the word "self" for a reason.

5. Now, just for fun, write down three indulgences you can realistically do this week to hone your Empress energy. They do not have to be related to your other journal prompts.

The Self-Care Equation

That little voice in your head? The one that says you can't, that tells you to stay quiet, the one that's always judging you? That little guy has to go. We know you've heard this before, and it's easier said than done. But it can be done! In fact, getting rid of that voice is a lot of what we're here to do. To make the big ideas that tarot, self-care, and creativity present cohesive and less overwhelming, we need to break them down in a way that is understandable, solvable, and achievable. That goal led us, believe it or not, to creating an equation that would help you understand the big ideas presented in each suit (and throughout this book) more clearly. The equation we developed looks like this, but feel free to sit with these ideas and futz with the equation to make it work for you. Ours looks like:

(Imagination + Reflection + Expression) - Judgment of Self = Creativity/Self-Care

What does that mean for us in the practical? How do we actually apply this to creative methods and our self-care practice? Let's explore that now.

1. Everything begins in your Imagination. Imagination is the seed that became The Empress's garden of abundance. Those ideas in your head, flashes of images, dreams, bits of nonsense—that's your imagination percolating, your imagination at play.

2. What do we *do* with all of the great visuals or ideas our imagination brings us? That's where Reflection comes in. Take some time to really look at those ideas, those flashing images. Reflect on an idea and you will hopefully see what the scope of it can be, or what it should look like in a more tangible format. Do *not* ask yourself, "How can the thing I imagined turn into a real thing?" Instead ask yourself, "Now that I've thought about it, what does it mean and why does it resonate for me?" This is the part that gets people hung up. Reflection takes time and grace.

   Reflection is a vital aspect of self-care. It is an aspect of rest, a necessary part of our journey. Rest heals, rest rejuvenates, and rest resets our mind. It also just feels good! There's a reason "well-rested" is a word that fills us with satisfaction. As we think about stepping back from the countless ideas our imagination spews out, it's important to remember we *are* stepping back. Magic has to percolate, and so does creativity. Imagine. Then reflect. In other words: play. Then rest.

3. Now we add Expression to Imagination and Reflection in our equation. Expression is the flavor of the piece. This is when we add in details that really make our work our own. These details might include your experience or point of view, how you've been impacted by the medium you're creating in, or it can be as simple as your unique spin on your medium or the tools you create with. This is why retellings or remakes can often be at least as good as or better than the originals—because of the creator's Expression.

4. Our equation continues with subtraction—get rid of that inner critic, by eradicating Judgment of Self from our creative equation. Sometimes when we add Imagination, Reflection, and Expression together, we come to conclusions that are uncomfortable for us. Maybe they are uncomfortable because they challenge who we thought we were. Maybe they are uncomfortable because the creative work seems to want to push the bounds of what is possible for us to say. Maybe they are uncomfortable because they are simply unexpected. In any case, the only way to approach creating authentically is to eradicate Judgment of Self.

This is the part that's easier said than done. We know that. It is also the part that will free you the most if you allow yourself to really let go of it. This book is a container for you to tackle whatever you want or need to tackle. If, by the end, you still are not comfortable sharing with the world at large, that's okay! Give yourself space to say or create whatever you need to say or create *now*—and just see how that changes your perspective.

When we release Judgment of Self, our selves and our creations thrive. It's in this hardest piece of the equation that we truly learn the most valuable lessons from The Empress.

Let's begin.

PART ONE

Preparing the Way
for The Empress

YOUR INNER EMPRESS

What do you do to care for yourself, nurture your creativity?

his question always stumps people, but we all have something. Some of us keep journals. Some of us spend a couple of lazy days each spring penning pastoral poetry. Some of us sing in the car, encourage the companies we work at to innovate, or send thoughtfully written greeting cards for the holidays. Maybe you daydream wildly and let that consume your walks around the block. Maybe you cook, bake, or mix any kind of drink to blow off steam. Maybe your apartment is a perfect mirror of your inner process that you created via design and imagination. These are all creative acts.

Spend some time before you go any further making notes about what you do that is creative. List it all out as it comes to you. As you go along, you'll realize that a lot of these activities are forms of self-care.

And self-care is the ultimate goal. Once you have your list, work to slowly expand both your creative activities and how you think about creativity. Pick up a forgotten hobby that used to bring you joy, or be more intentional when you do the things you already do. Jot down new ideas as they come to you— because they *will* come to you once you tune in a bit more.

In this book, you'll find that we've provided many prompts and rituals as we work through the lessons from The Empress. You can take the rituals and prompts as they come, creating many small projects that may or may not ever be cohesive. Or, maybe you've got a few projects you want to play with as you go, and you can use the prompts and rituals to move yourself further ahead. You may also choose to work on one big project, incorporating the prompts into a world you've already designed.

Ways to Engage Your Creative Inner Empress for Self-Care

- Use your tarot cards! Ask the cards for inspiration or pull some cards and sit with them to see what pops up in terms of both self-care and creativity.

- Do some freewriting or trance writing.

- Take in some good art or fun media. Then write some notes or journal your responses to it.

- Brainstorm ideas for food, travel, gift-giving, or anything else that inspires you and makes you think in new ways. Try brainstorming with a friend or partner as well. I love seeing what different brains and hearts inspire me to think of, and I absolutely love when ideas come together for something altogether new.

- Try something new creatively. If you normally bake, try writing a poem. If you normally write poems, grab some sculptor's clay and see what happens.

- Try something new in general! Most of us have a bucket list of places we'd like to see and things we'd like to do. Next time you feel restless, actually stop what you're doing and go see or do something from that list.

- Put up a social media post asking people what last inspired them creatively (or just inspired them to get their lust for life back). Make an effort to try at least one thing someone shares.

- Try a guided meditation that leaves space for you to imagine what happens (as opposed to one that walks you through every step of the way).

- Write a letter to a loved one. Not an email or a DM; an actual pen-to-paper letter.

- Make something totally new, without a strict recipe for dinner tonight. (Recipe formulas are fine because they leave space for you to play and timing matters with so much cooking.)

- Sketch out some symbols or images from your dreams last night. Yes, even if you "can't draw."

- Use this list as a jumping-off point to come up with your own ways to unlock this part of yourself. The goal here is not necessarily to create something yet, but to simply engage that imaginative and expressive part of yourself.

Introducing The Empress: A Tarot Spread

What better way to get to know The Empress than through the tarot itself? This spread is designed to help you ease into this book and get to know the spirit of The Empress. Instead of thinking of The Empress as something outside of ourselves, let's think about The Empress as an aspect of self. We have access to them; they live within us. We are able to express ourselves fully, to nurture ourselves, and to create just as much as The Empress does.

Don't worry—if you are totally new to tarot, feel free to read ahead and return to this spread later!

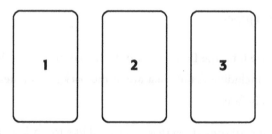

Card 1: You, now. What does your self-care practice look like now?

Card 2: What is your current relationship to your inner Empress?

Card 3: How will you grow as you read this book?

Opening Ritual: Dedication

The Empress is dedicated to their personal growth, and they are also committed and loyal. This is a side of them that emerges when it comes to taking care of ourselves; The Empress sees us all as deserving of love, worthy of the freedom to express ourselves openly. The Empress within is also an incredibly encouraging figure, there to help us commit to self-love. How can you dedicate yourself to this ritual act of loving?

Throughout this book, you will be encouraged to experiment with ritual. The rituals will gradually get more complex, until you are comfortable casting a full circle and working within a more ceremonial framework. But sometimes the simplest rituals are the most powerful. Sometimes they are exactly what you need.

The purpose of this ritual is to create a sense of ease and curiosity.

Materials:

- The Empress card from your tarot deck (or a printed image, if you don't have your own deck yet)

- This book

- A slip of paper

Step One: Gaze into The Empress card. Really connect with them. Look at every detail—including details that are in the background, details that you hadn't noticed before.

Step Two: Think of something that you would like to work on in the course of this book. Is there a particular creative project? Is there a feeling of self-love that you would like to cultivate? Picture that clearly. Imagine it taking the form of light in your body. Pick up the piece of paper and imagine that this dedication is flowing out of your hands and onto the page.

Step Three: If you would like to solidify your intention for working through this book, put it into words. One sentence will do. It could be something like "I will learn to express myself freely," or "I will cultivate a new form of creativity." Write your intention on the paper.

Step Four: Use this slip of paper as a bookmark as you are reading. This will serve as an anchor, a guidepost for you as you move forward.

2

THE BASICS OF TAROT
FOR SELF-CARE

arot, put simply, is a deck of seventy-eight cards commonly used in divination. Divination can mean communicating with Self and Spirit, and it can also mean getting a bird's-eye view or new outlook on a situation that has us stumped. There's a lot of mystique around the tarot deck, but some of it is unnecessary. To get past that mystique and to help you unblock any resistance to working with the tarot, approach the deck simply as cards with pictures. The pictures tell you a story and give you a message. And that collection of messages can be used in inquiry or divination.

When Cassandra writes about tarot, it's important to them to remember that its roots go back *way* before the Rider-Waite-Smith Tarot. The first extant tarot decks were printed between 1440 and 1450 in Italy. The first one we think of when we think of early tarot decks is the *Tarot de Marseille*, which was popular in 17th century France. These early decks were used first as a card game, and then people decided to add some parlor mystery to them by "reading" them. These decks were likely inspired by art in castles, museums, and other Very Notable Buildings.

It is also extremely worth noting that Pamela Colman Smith, who illustrated the famed Rider-Waite-Smith Tarot in 1909, was deeply influenced by paintings and engravings of the *Sola Busca Tarot*, a 15th-century deck that she may have seen featured at the British Museum just a couple of years before the Rider-Waite-Smith was created and published. This influence is undeniable (just Google the Ten of Wands or Three of Swords from each), but to her credit Smith was likely viewing these as pieces of art. Smith was deeply intuitive, but she prided herself on being an artist first. Similarly, the *Thoth Tarot Deck* wouldn't have coming into being without the creative genius of the artist Lady Frieda Harris.

The tarot literally cannot exist without artists illustrating the deck even in the present day. It just cannot. This might seem rudimentary or obvious but so many tarot writers have worked so hard to write about these seventy-eight pieces of art as cards with set meaning that we've forgotten that this process is (and should be) art first. Even if you are primarily interested in learning the tarot traditionally, focusing on the visual aspect of your deck *is* the secret way in.

How to Read a Tarot Card When You Know Nothing about Tarot Cards

With that in mind, let's explore the tarot cards. The tarot deck is seventy-eight pieces of artwork, seventy-nine if you count the guidebook as a piece of literary art. That means we should explore its roots as art to help divine card meanings and interpretations for ourselves. You don't need to have a full knowledge to get started; you just need some tips to get your interpretive juices flowing. This section of our workbook covers art appreciation as your path to tarot interpretation, a method we maintain is *the* best starting point for personal tarot understanding, queering the tarot, and yes, using the tarot for self-care, self-love, and creative purposes.

It's so much easier to get started than people think! In the same way that we are all creative—be honest—we are all critics too. When you see a play or a movie, I guarantee you spend time with your friends dissecting what you loved, what you hated, and what you thought about it. When you see a piece of visual art, whether consciously or not, you probably ask yourself what you're looking at. Once you have an idea of what you're looking at, you probably (again, consciously or not) figure out what else it makes you think about, how you feel about it, and how it connects to other things you've seen or experienced in your life. That's all you need to do to the individual tarot cards before you start reading them for yourself!

Let's Practice!

Pull out a tarot card, and just sit with it at first. How do you feel? What emotions are coming up? Once you have that, take note of it. Now, play with the following ideas, taking notes when appropriate.

- First, what pieces of the image stick out to you? What is the first thing you see? How does that strike you? If you know *why* it strikes you, take note of that, too.

- Next, unfocus your eyes so the image gets blurry and see what you still notice or see.

- Refocus your eyes: what is newly sharp and crisp to you?

- From there, start describing the card. You can say it out loud or write it down, but don't just think it. You'll rush if you do. As you do so, what action do you notice happening in the card? How might that indicate a piece of advice, an action step, or a thought process for a reading?

- Now, start breaking down the image into smaller pieces and symbols. What do these colors, these symbols, these characters, and actions mean? What else can you mine for along this vein? (You can research the commonly accepted interpretations of these symbols, but I strongly encourage you to take the time to think about what they mean to you first.)

- Think about your specific deck and any changes the creator made. For example, in *The Numinous Tarot*, creator Cedar McCloud uses Tomes instead of Pentacles. What do "books" and "tomes," "libraries," and other associated words mean to you, *and* how does that compare to how you see the more common Pentacles or Disks?

Theorize on why any changes were made, what stands out about the card you're looking at versus any other card of the same name in a different deck, and take notes on all of that as well.

- Finally, check the guidebook that came with your deck! What does the deck creator or author point out that you missed? How does that change or add to your current understanding of the card?

After this exercise, pull a new card and run through these questions again, with deeper intention. Ask the card a specific question. Go through all the above steps. This targeted reading will give you guidance specific to the question you asked.

Do this above exercise regularly to stretch and strengthen the muscles you'll use in your blossoming tarot practice. With practice, reading will get faster and easier over time and will eventually become second nature. The deck's guidebook should merely provide keywords or messages as a jumping off point. Practice seeing the cards as stand-alone pieces of art—which are both the fruit of the tarot creator's inspiration and the creative seeds for your own expression.

The Basic Tarot Structure

We can demystify the tarot further by breaking down the five sets or groups of cards that exist within it, called suits. Tarot has deep roots as a card game. This means tarot is supposed to be fun and learnable—but games do have rules and best strategies. The point of tarot books is often to offer best strategies and suggested rules for divining, but these systems do go back to the deck's gaming days. Here is an incredibly brief overview of what each suit represents when we read, teach, or study tarot. We'll also look at some other important information about your deck.

The Major Arcana are the cards labeled 0 through 21 and have a word or short phrase like "The Fool," "The Lovers," or "Judgment" on them. These cards hold the element of Spirit, and therefore they deal with major occult ideas, our personal gnosis, and highest ideals and contain the bigger picture of our lives and beyond. To understand the Majors in terms of self-care, this might mean taking time for spirituality, to probe those big existential questions, or to process major life events and synthesize their lessons (and how you've grown). In terms of creating, this is where we see the groundwork for creation and storytelling laid bare. For example, many refer to the Fool's Journey as a story of how we create our lives.

Each suit of the Minor Arcana connects to an element:

- The **Wands** typically connect to **Fire** and all the beauty fire entails. Wands are passion, potential, action, gut instinct, sensual pleasures, and anything that gets us out of bed in the morning. When we think of self-care and Wands, we think about trying to avoid burnout, following our muse and our passions, and trusting our gut instinct. They also represent raw creativity. This is the Imagination piece of the equation from the intro. These cards act quickly, so in terms of creating, this is the suit that gives you those flashes of inspiration that you need to act on *stat* lest they fly away.

- The **Swords** mainly connect to **Air** and represent logic, technology, science, systems, and processes. They often represent institutions and the harm that institutions do, but they are also our ability to overcome that harm. Communication and words are frequently lumped in with this suit, and I've even heard it called the Writer's Suit. Swords remind us to take care of ourselves when we're hurting, show us how tools and technology can enable us to take better care of ourselves, and encourage us to use the most logical approach when able to make things easier on ourselves. When we turn to creating, Swords can help us turn our pain outward into our creative pursuits. They can also help us fine-tune our skill set for creative work that is strong and accomplished. In our equation for creativity, the Swords represent the Reflection piece, both because they are the part of the tarot that advises discernment and because of their strong connection to the mind.

- The **Cups** connect to **Water,** which can correlate to relationships, emotions, and healing journeys. Cups are about our relationships with ourselves too, not simply our relationships with others. When we look at creativity as an act of self-care, both that act and the art that we create from that place of self-care are held gently here. Later in this workbook, we look at the Cups as a journey of gaining confidence in expressing ourselves. Self-expression is one of the primary goals of Cups, and from there we can even progress into expressing other pieces of knowledge or ideas we're holding on to tightly. When it comes to self-care, this suit encourages us to spend time doing things we love with people we love and indulging our inner child.

- Finally, we have the steadfast **Pentacles**, which connect to **Earth.** It's easy to look at these cards as being about money and career, and they can certainly reference both of those things. Pentacles are the world and Earth itself and can also represent the materia with which we cast spells and create. Cups are the thing we end up creating, but Pentacles are the paint and canvas that artwork is created out of. Another facet of Pentacles we'll explore is sustainability. This suit can help you build a realistic and practical plan to keep up a creative practice that brings you joy and the ability to create regularly. Finally, Pentacles often represent the human body and therefore embodiment. It's here where we can, as Mary Oliver would say, "let the soft animal of our body love what it loves," and begin releasing Judgment of Self for doing so.

Tarot and Story

The tarot further encourages self-care because each individual tarot image helps us tell our stories. Every creator needs a steady input of art, idea, and story in order to be inspired and energized. The tarot provides plenty. The section on the suits goes deeply into their stories and various story structures, but I'll add a few notes here, too.

Stories do not need to be linear! Some cards can represent memory, dream sequences, or premonitions in the story you are thinking of telling. Be open-minded as to the flow of the cards, even if you're working with them in order. Self-discovery is not a linear process, and your own creative journey is ever flowing. Don't get too caught up in what that is "supposed to" look like.

Many literary scholars think stories need a beginning, a middle, and an end. Many disagree. Indigenous storytellers have a rich oracular history of telling stories that do not unfold with a beginning, middle, and end. They leave lots of room for ambiguity and further exploration and creation in a number of their stories. Decide for yourself what makes something a story, and what those structures do and do not look like for you. That can and should be flexible, but knowing what basic structures work for you (or not) will make your job as a creator a lot easier.

Some people think there are no new stories. We disagree. There are infinite new ways to *tell* any story. When you're working from your own point of view, it's going to be important and unique, even if you are retelling an existing story through your own lens. Your voice, story, what you've learned, how you've learned what you learned, your identity, and relationships: these are the things this book will tap into and what will set your work apart.

Most creative output is telling a story. A dancer is telling a story with their dance. A painter is showing a still moment of a bigger story, if they aren't painting a whole story. A baker bakes a loaf of bread to share with others in a futuristic story about community building or family bonding. You don't always need to tell the whole story in your creative work. It might not even make sense to do so. Many stories unfold on their own from your subconscious and teach you something you weren't even aware of. Embrace your personal story.

Pull a couple of tarot cards and using only what we've talked about so far (and anything else you already know about tarot), see how they connect to your personal story. This will help you both pinpoint and expand what you are hoping to express and will help you understand what story is and can be when you're working with the tarot.

The Elephant in the Room

Something that troubles people in tarot, witchcraft, and occultism is how common interpretations lean deeply into the importance of gender binary and hierarchy. You might even be wondering why two non-binary people are writing a book about a card often ascribed to traditional femininity and motherhood. We both have endless things to say about gender, but we'll keep it to two ideas for the purposes of our work here. For these reasons and beyond, we are referring to The Empress as "they" throughout this book.

"Male" and "female" are modern concepts in occultism and witchcraft whereas occultism and witchcraft are ageless. Before "male and female" we most likely said something like "passive and active" or "creative and reactive." Please note that we are *not* trying to rewrite masculinity and femininity. Rather, we are suggesting that while we often can't get away from binaries in the tarot, we can push them away from the social construct of gender and introduce new ways to think about contrasting energies.

Take a second to think about what contrasting energies you hold or struggle with. As you approach creative work, think about integrating those dualities instead of the prescribed ones. Where do you see those binaries in your work? Where do you see all the space in between and beyond them in your tarot deck?

This is a book on creating and self-expression and on reclaiming these things as self-care. So if a gender or hierarchy doesn't work for you even if you try to rewrite it, guess what? You get to chuck it out the window for *at least* this book's process. Whew, feel better?

One way we can break past gender in the Court Cards specifically, as well as work more deeply with the elements (which we will explore more deeply in this book), is by learning the common understanding of the elements associated with each Court Card.

- Pages are often thought of as the Earth element.

- Knights most often correlate to Air.

- Queens regularly correlate to Water.

- Kings are usually regarded as Fire.

This means that the Page of Wands can be read as "Earth of Fire." You read this by using what you know of Earth, say steadfastness for example, and thinking about how that interacts with Fire. In this case, that means that you may see this page as someone or something who stabilizes the unpredictability of fire. Refer to the following chart of double elementation for easy reference.

	Wands	Cups	Swords	Pentacles
King	fire/fire	fire/water	fire/air	fire/earth
Queen	water/fire	water/water	water/air	water/earth
Knight	air/fire	air/water	air/air	air/earth
Page	earth/fire	earth/water	earth/air	earth/earth

• • •

Now let's talk about the inherent hierarchy present in the Court Cards and many of the Majors. When I see cards as hierarchical, I like to set them in a circle with surrounding cards instead of a line to try to break through that. For example, if we see The Emperor, Empress, and Hierophant as too hierarchical to deal with easily, set them in a circle with The Fool through The Lovers. In a circle, we see how each card flows into the next one and learns from the previous one. Move your circle around too, so no one card sits at the top or bottom, and do the same exercise again. This works for your Court Cards, too, which is another card grouping people have trouble grappling with for this reason.

In the case of gender and hierarchy, you can approach it any way that genuinely works for you. We've already told you that you can just chuck the whole notion of gender. You can do the above exercise with hierarchy to just chuck it as well. However, we do live in a society where gender and hierarchy are ever-present. Not only are they present, but they also create privilege and lack, drive home a scarcity mindset, and create profound oppression that we often internalize. An equally modern approach is doing the hard work of recognizing that although these things might be constructs, they are also very real in our society. You would then use these cards to recognize when you were dealing with something that gender or hierarchy contributes to, giving you more information to help you handle it.

As you navigate the tarot, you will find things that challenge you for all the right reasons because that's what tarot does. You'll be asked to free yourself from self-judgment, to express emotions you've been repressing, and to embrace the unknown. Scary, but important. That is so often what brilliant creation and innovative witchy thought are born from. This book exists to hold space for that process, and tarot has a way of parsing the hard messages into easier step-by-step ones.

That being said, you might find things that challenge you for the wrong reasons. If something comes up that is harming your ability to create, don't use it. No matter your reasons. We're book authors, not your parents or therapist. You do not need permission from us or anyone to disregard something that is harmful to your process. Just chuck it. We not only encourage, but also applaud this! Learning tarot and using it to carve out space for self-care and creativity is a process you do at your own pace, on your own terms. We are simply here to help.

Choosing a Tarot Deck

A lot of would-be tarot readers get stuck in the "finding a deck" part of the process, but it can be so easy! To help with creation and inspiration, this is all you need to do:

- Find art that draws you in. When you can get lost in a card because of its art, your intuition will take over and your whole process will be smoother. Art has the power to move us in ways that don't need words. You want art that will speak to you directly, that will awaken something within you.

- Pick a deck whose messages and art are clear to you or a deck that comes with a guidebook you really like. Don't make it harder than it has to be—there are countless decks out there, and any number of them are perfect for you! Pick the easiest one that meets your needs.

Treat the deck like a first date that is cute but not so cute you trip over your own tongue. Bear with us on this—we know it's corny. Dates like this should be approached with interest and curiosity. You shouldn't be married to an outcome or worried about what's next. You should simply be getting to know this "person" and telling them a little bit about you as it comes up. It really can be this sweet, and you'll learn so much more about the cards and about yourself when you approach it that way.

Once you have your deck, spend some time exploring it. Look at each image individually. Spread suits out and look at them as a story, in order. We walk you through this in each section of this book, but doing it on your own is likely to inspire you before we even jump in. Do some gentle shuffling; play with some three-card draws or simple spreads. While tarot expertise is not an expectation of this book, you'll feel more confident creating from the tarot if you spend some time exploring it. Remember to keep an open mind and have fun—nothing we do here is meant to burden or overwhelm you.

3

TAROT AND RITUAL

"Magic is made in the margins." – Pam Grossman

ach tarot card is an initiation to a deeper level of understanding and a key to unlock our secrets. The word *arcana* means "things that are secret or mysterious." The tarot is broken down into Major Arcana and Minor Arcana—known as greater secrets and smaller secrets. The secrets of the Major Arcana have to do with esoteric, spiritual, and archetypal matters. The secrets of the Minor Arcana are more mundane and relate to our everyday lives and environment. In this way the tarot links esoteric and material, much like ritual does. Magical ritual is built into the tarot in some truly fascinating ways, from the structure of the deck itself to the archetypes that it presents and to the rituals we develop to help us read the cards. But we can also use tarot magically to draw on the energy of those archetypes, or as an inspiration for how we want to show up in the world. That's why there are rituals and spells sprinkled throughout this book.

First Things First: What Do We Mean by Ritual?

We all use many rituals throughout our lives, little rituals that help us as we move through our days. Perhaps it's making coffee first thing in the morning, or choosing our outfit the night before, or wearing your favorite shirt whenever your favorite team is playing. Maybe one of your rituals is getting a fancy coffee on Wednesdays. Rituals are habits and actions that we take to give ourselves support and love.

Magical ritual takes these things deeper, elevating them to a symbolic level and creating change around you. Magical ritual is a ritual with purpose. We design magical rituals because we want something different, we want something to happen, or we simply want to explore new ideas in a systematic way. Ritual doesn't have to be elaborate and complicated. Ritual—*your* ritual—is designed to hold space for your self-care and creative process.

To create a magical ritual or spell, first you decide on your desired outcome. Then consider what symbols and objects make sense to work with and the actions that you want to take. Then create a ritual outline. The actions in a magical ritual often mirror larger actions that we want to happen in the mundane world. You start with an intention of what you would like to happen, and then the actions you take represent those things happening more broadly. This process is a way of developing ritual theatre, of creating a container that mirrors the outcomes you want to gain from ritual. For example, let's say you want to break through imposter syndrome regarding your self-expression. You could create a ritual where you write all of the things that feed into your imposter syndrome on a piece of paper and then you burn the paper. The first ritual action (writing everything down) represents getting that out of your head, and therefore outside yourself. Burning the paper then represents destroying those insecurities or transforming them into something different. Then, over the next few days, pay attention to how you feel and what opportunities come your way over the next several months.

I have a confession to make: I have often struggled to stick to a daily ritual, or a daily habit. I'll go on a meditation jag for a month, and then fall off the wagon, terrified to get back on because I'm not perfect. But perfection isn't the goal of ritual— **support is the goal of ritual.** *The more often you engage in rituals—whether that is pulling a semi-daily tarot card or lighting your altar candle—the more natural they will feel. Daily rituals have the power to become second nature.*

This chapter is intended to help you create rituals and feel confident engaging with the ritual sections of this book.

Building a Daily Tarot and Self-Care Ritual

Ritual Structure One

Whether you are a seasoned tarot reader or a student just beginning your Fool's Journey, pulling a daily card is a really good way of centering and grounding yourself. Pull a card in the morning, perhaps after lighting some altar candles. Take a moment to look at the card. Let yourself get lost in the art of the card and make a few notes about what you see there. One of Siri's favorite fellow witches, Lara Veleda Vesta, recommends a nonnegotiable ten minute ritual daily. She also recommends "frontloading" your daily ritual by doing it first thing in the morning. This accomplishes two things: (1) it shows dedication and priority; and (2) it means that you don't have to worry about that ritual for the rest of the day.

Ritual Structure Two

Some people struggle to create healthy routines for their self-care. Some people struggle to create healthy routines for their self-care, but you are worth the time and effort it takes to establish them. If you struggle to remember to do your daily practice (whatever it may be), when you remember you can stop what you're doing and do it right then. Carry your tarot deck with you throughout the day so that you can pull a card when you remember. A friend of Siri's recommended the "two day" rule when it comes to building habits. It's okay to forget your daily ritual for a day, but then it's extra important to do it the next day. Two days off disrupts the flow of building the habit.

Above all:
Your daily tarot ritual should be something you look forward to doing.

This will make the ritual "stick." If it's something that you actively look forward to, it's more likely that you will keep doing it. The more you engage with your cards, the easier it will be to read them and learn them. When we add tarot to creative life, it can help by clarifying the direction we need to take, or it can just be a really good way to memorize card meanings naturally. Adding a bit of magic to your daily tarot pull can make it even more exciting.

Ritual Structure Three

Ground your magical rituals in very tactile things: A specific candle, a crystal, an anointing oil. Sometimes that thing becomes the ritual itself—lighting the candle, holding the crystal, anointing yourself with oil. But ritual always starts because you want to help shift something in your mind. Ritual also helps our memory to connect our creative processes with something physical to create a ritual around them. Lighting a candle is my favorite way of doing this. If you have one particular project that you're working through for this book, choose a candle with a scent that will remind you of the project. Light the candle, pull a tarot card, and you are already in the mindset for your creative session.

> Take a moment to think about what a supportive daily ritual would look like for you, and how you can build tarot into your daily ritual. Jot down a few ideas. Let yourself get creative! Choose one of these rituals and begin practicing to see how it feels.

Ritual Structure Four

Create an altar.

Altar magic is one of those things that is incredibly subtle, but it can become an essential aspect of ritual for you. An altar is basically a space in your home that acts as a magical container and conduit for your spiritual growth. Different magical traditions might have different uses for altars, and they might suggest that you have specific things on the altar. We know many witches who have dedicated altars for deities they work with or for ancestor work as well as more generic altars. These altars will incorporate different images or items that remind you of your ancestors or that particular deity, while a generic altar will house all kinds of symbols specific to your current workings.

During the writing of this book, Siri built a mini altar to The Empress on their desk, including their favorite Empress card and several stones for creativity. You might put a crow feather on an altar for the Morrighan or a rose for Aphrodite. Of course, an altar can be any size. If you don't have space for an altar, if you're traveling a lot, if you have kids (or cats) that will disrupt your altar, it's totally okay to put it in a small tin, box, or otherwise portable option. Siri has used leftover tins from mints in the past.

. . . .

We highly recommend that you create an altar dedicated to self-care and self-expression for the duration of reading this book.

. . . .

One of our favorite tarot cards to use for this (other than The Empress) is The Lovers card. Personally, this card has been more helpful as a card representing self-care and self-commitment than as a card about romantic love. The *Next World Tarot* has one of our favorite depictions of The Lovers card. It shows a person, fully dressed in their punk outfit, looking in a mirror. They use a mobility aid, and you can tell that they have some chronic health issues going on. They are looking into a mirror, and out of the mirror steps a naked version of themselves, handing them spoons (a common metaphor for the energy of disabled folks). When Siri was working on some really deep self-love stuff, they took this card out of the tarot deck and placed it on an altar dedicated to self-love.

That is one powerful example of how we can build altars around tarot cards. We recommend that you use only one card for your first tarot altar—that way the energy is a little more clear to you, and you can really connect with that specific card. The most obvious choice for this book is The Empress, but you do you. Once you've chosen the tarot card that you want to focus on, take some extra time to gaze at the card and determine what other symbols would be good on the altar itself. For example, if you were looking at that specific version of The Lovers, perhaps put a spoon on the altar, or roses, or anything else that reminds you of the self-love you want to bring into your life.

The most important aspect of building an altar is your personal connection to it. Your altar is for you. Please don't pressure yourself to have Instagram-worthy altars. This is for you, not for anyone else's consumption. We also want to reiterate that you don't have to have traditional items on your altar. For example, a traditional Wiccan altar usually includes a chalice, an athame, a wand, and statue representations of the threefold goddess and the horned god. Unless this imagery speaks to you (and perhaps unless you are Wiccan), you do not need to follow this directive! On altars for self-love, we have definitely put items like The Lovers card, rose petals, a rose quartz, a piece of paper with my intention for building self-love on it, a mirror, and so much more. You get to choose what your altar looks like, because your altar will help you to create magic.

4

TAROT AND ELEMENTAL MAGIC

o understand how to work with your Tarot deck magically, to use it to create magical transformation, let's consider briefly the five elements and the suits of the tarot. Most of the tarot rituals in this book will have to do with the elements, because they are a very tangible way of organizing our magic. Elemental energy is important to take into consideration when crafting ritual, and it is even more important when we are considering tarot for magic.

The five elements are essential to understanding a lot of occult thought, and each of these elements is present in a different aspect of the Tarot. Each of these elements heightens specific areas of self-care and self-expression.

The Five Elements Are Fire, Air, Water, Earth, and Spirit

Spirit relates to the Major Arcana, as discussed earlier in this book. The element of Spirit permeates the biggest transitions, aha moments, and challenges of life. Spirit is always with you, a support. It makes up your identity and how you see the world. Awakening the spirit within means understanding our own spirits as being in conversation with the spirits of everything around us. This is the great connecting force of the universe. In the Major Arcana section of this workbook, we talk about how the Major Arcana is made up of the "Big

Life Lessons" we learn. Magically, Spirit is present when we bring our whole selves to ritual. Spirit can also represent literal spirits—house spirits, spirits of the dead, fae spirits, land spirits, and so forth. So when working with this element, bringing the larger, more universal energy of Spirit (or the Major Arcana's archetypes) can really help you to connect with an entire world of guides.

That leaves four elements related to the four suits of the Minor Arcana.

- **Fire:** Wands—Passion, Excitement, Transformation, Drive, Inspiration

- **Air:** Swords—Clarity, Intelligence, Mental Health, Healing from Trauma, Communication

- **Water:** Cups—Healing, Intuition, Heart, Relationships, Love, Emotions

- **Earth:** Pentacles—Stability, Career, Home, Family, Nurturing

If you've been studying the tarot for a bit, you'll notice that these are the primary themes that come up in each of the suits. Of course, at the top of each section of our Minor Arcana chapters, we will cover this in more detail. For your self-care practice, become sensitive to how you internally hold or express each elemental quality: they can be in balance or out of balance. This self-awareness will inform how you work with the tarot.

Fire

Fire is usually associated with the Wands in Tarot. Magically, fire represents transformation and action moving forward. Fire can also be used for destruction. Candle magic, bonfire magic, or any type of ritual burning is an important aspect of fire magic. We use this element when we want a change to occur. This is why candle magic is so very universal—the candle is a spark, a charge of energy that initiates a change you are seeking. Why do magic if you're perfectly satisfied with everything? Working with charged ritual candles can help you to take your magic to the next level in a really powerful way.

Fire is the thing that gets us moving. It is the aspect of our Self that propels our forward motion, the source of passion.

- **When in balance:** Moving toward your dreams, inspired, energized, standing up for yourself, fighting for what you believe in

- **When out of balance:** Sluggish, dispassionate, unable to move forward, stuck, no "fight" in you

- **Traditional Fire offerings for the altar:** Candles, fiery stones like carnelian (when sustainably sourced), lantern/oil lamp, wand

- **Journal prompt:** How do you find Fire energy showing up in your life?

Air

Air is associated with the Swords in tarot. Air is all about mental acuity, technology, and communication. Swords cut deep to the truth, and that is their primary focus: Truth, with that capital T. Often that means looking at the ugly side of Truth, in order to heal. The word that we use most often to talk about air magic is "clarity." Air makes our rituals clearer, it helps us to refine our goals, and it helps us to communicate what needs to be communicated. If you're doing magic that involves casting a circle, call in Air first because it will help you communicate with the other elements and entities you are invoking.

Air is all around us, but we can't see it. It is the breath that supports our life and the vehicle for our voices. This connection with communication and speech makes Air the element of mental activity, as well as mental illness and healing from trauma.

- **When in balance:** Communication is clear, mind is clear, feeling inspired and capable of creating something

- **When out of balance:** Difficulty communicating, hard time making decisions, lots of trauma response

- **Traditional Air offerings for the altar:** Incense, feathers, "airy" plants like a dandelion that has gone to seed, knife

- **Journal prompt:** How do you find Air energy showing up in your life?

Water

Water is of course related to Cups. Water flows; it adapts to fill the container that you put it in. Water is also one of the most powerful elements of healing we have available to us. Water is healing not just on a physical level but also on an interpersonal and soul level. In the tarot, Cups often rule our relationships. This raises the question of how we heal one another, how we can show love and trust to one another, and what the impact of that is on our overall well-being. The Cups have incredible stories embedded within their suit; they help us learn what kinds of relationships work best for us, they tell a story about the healing journey, and so much more.

Water is receptive and mutable, helping to cradle you in dark or difficult times and nourishing you in good times. This is also the element that connects us with the unconscious realm and therefore opens up our psychic capabilities.

- **When in balance:** Emotionally connected with others, feeling the love, supportive dreams, intuitive skills, psychic boundaries

- **When out of balance:** Mood swings, emotionally numb, distancing yourself from others, nightmares, feeling "cut off" from intuition, psychic debris

- **Traditional Water offerings for the altar:** Offering bowl and water, shells, anointing oil, water gathered from a place sacred to you

- **Journal prompt:** How do you find Water energy showing up in your life?

Earth

Earth energy is stability and comfort, knowing that you have enough and knowing where your power comes from. The suit of Pentacles follows this theme and teaches us how to build our lives mindfully. So often, this suit gets reduced down to "money matters" (which Siri rants about later). But it is so much more than that! The suit of Pentacles helps us to find the ground beneath our feet and build a legacy. This is especially beautiful for creatives who want to avoid burnout. Pentacles can help us focus, build the skills that we need, and plan for the long term.

Earth is solid ground beneath our feet. It is abundant, steadfast, and sturdy. This is the element that helps us follow through on all our fiery desires. It is also the provider, the reminder that we are okay, and we will be okay. This is an element of survival.

- **When in balance:** Grounded, connected, generous, stable, follow through, attention for details

- **When out of balance:** Stubborn, flighty, disorganized, difficulty making decisions, lack of confidence

- **Traditional Earth offerings for the altar:** Stones, rocks, crystals (ethically sourced), dirt, plants, herbs

- **Journal prompt:** How do you find Earth energy showing up in your life?

Magical Principles and Ritual Help

Witchcraft and tarot are powerful tools that you can use to further your understanding of yourself. That's why we're including sections at the end of each tarot-specific chapter to walk you through a ritual or spell that will help you connect to self-care and self-expression. These rituals will connect to the element of that suit, and they will be highly customizable in case you want to shift them a bit for your purposes. We take a highly DIY attitude to our own magic and encourage you to do the same. But there are some principles that are helpful to understand before doing any magic.

1. **You get out of magic what you put into it.**

   This is a good rule of thumb for most things in life, to be perfectly honest. You need to put in some effort in order to get good results—especially in magic. Of course, this does not mean that you need to push all of your energy behind your spellwork. We don't want to exhaust you. But it's definitely not helpful to show up in ritual and half-ass your way through.

   We're asking one thing from you in the ritual aspect of this book: trust yourself.

   Let go of those rational assumptions that magic doesn't work. Let go of the worry that you're doing it wrong. Just let yourself do it.

2. **We work with tarot cards, plants, crystals, and other objects in our magic because they are our allies.**

   One of the most fulfilling aspects of both of our spiritual beliefs is animism. This is the belief that plants, inanimate objects, and even natural phenomena have a soul of their own. Understanding that the items you use in the spell are friendly, that they are allies that lend their power to your magic, can be really helpful in believing in yourself and your magic.

   Additionally, we have several rituals listed in this book. If you want to gather the materials necessary for doing the rituals, flip to page 171, Appendix 1: Materia, for an extended list of items you can work with.

3. **Use the present tense when setting intentions.**

   It's always important to start your rituals with an intention. Otherwise, why are you doing it in the first place? We recommend that you set intentions in the present tense, because it creates a stronger connection between where you are now and where you want to be. The intention should also be specific, without being too specific. You'll know when you've got the right intention. Examples we used when writing this book were, "This book is being published through Weiser," and, "We are both satisfied with the outcomes of this book."

4. **Pay attention to how you feel before and after working magic.**

This will give you some really helpful guideposts for knowing whether your ritual or spell was successful. Often, there's a subtle (or not so subtle) shift in energy after having worked some magic. The easier it is for you to place your feelings, to identify where you feel them in your body, the easier it will be for you to see if anything has changed, and then to see how it has changed.

Some people struggle to identify feelings, and that's okay. Going through the journal prompts, or even doing a quick check-in with your tarot deck after your ritual will help you to identify those emotions. Don't be afraid to use your tarot deck!

The specific things you need to understand for working certain spells are detailed in those sections of the book.

5

TAROT SPREADS TO KICK-START YOUR JOURNEY

Now that you've thought about creativity, tarot magic, and what it all means for you, it's time to get your cards out and lay some groundwork for your creative process. This will mean interpreting the cards—the thing that we've been leading up to this whole time!

Hopefully, you've already started your daily tarot practice—pulling one card for each day. Now you're feeling ready to move on to reading with more than one card. Reading tarot in a spread is helpful when you want a little bit more than one card will give you. The cards talk to each other, revealing new and important facets of a situation that you might not get with one card alone.

It's really useful to see these readings as a conversation. You are able to ask multiple questions, and the cards will answer. This also helps to facilitate that deeper connection with your deck. When I'm reading cards in a spread, here's my basic guideline:

- What seems to be the overall theme of the spread?

- Is one suit prevalent here, or is the reading fairly well balanced?

- When you read the cards in the spread placements, are there cards that seem to be in direct conversation with one another?

This will help you to feel comfortable and confident reading the following spreads for yourself. First, we'll give you some spreads for self-care, and then we'll move into spreads that act as creative prompts.

When Cassandra was getting their theatre degree, their professors really hammered home the right way to read a play as a theatre artist:

- You read it once just to read it, just to see what it is and what it has to offer.

- You read it a second time to read for your role (which includes reading it with director, producer, marketing, or tech designer eyes).

- You read it a third time to get specific about your role, look for the details, nuance, and creative sparks you may have missed.

- Then you read it one more time before you begin making plans. In this reading, you're letting your own ideas and notes take shape. You're visualizing as you read, watching the play come to life in your mind.

For the purposes of *Lessons from the Empress,* this isn't a bad approach to reading a tarot spread. Read through it a few different times, assuring that you're seeing your role in the reading spring to life, watching as the reading takes shape with visuals and ideas.

Spreads for Self-Care

Mind, Body, Soul Reading

This is the perfect introduction to reading tarot in spread form and is a really good way of checking in with yourself in the present moment and getting clear on what you need.

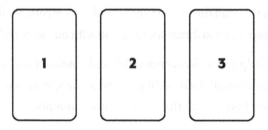

Card 1: Mind—This is a card that tells you how your mental health is at the moment. This card is also sometimes associated with the past, a.k.a. memories that may be coming back for you.

Card 2: Body—This is the card of the present moment, how you are feeling in your body and what your body needs. Very often, this is a card that indicates where we need some healing.

Card 3: Soul—The Soul card is aspirational. I often think of this card as a message from our higher self, a card that connects us to the Divine. This can help us see the bigger picture.

Unblocking Yourself Spread

This might look like a simple spread, but it can deliver really intense information right from the start. This spread is particularly good for when you are feeling afraid to show up as yourself, or when you feel like you're not able to advocate for yourself in your life.

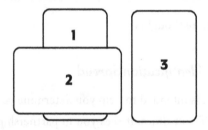

Card 1: The thing you want to express—This is the aspect of yourself that is most important to bring forward—the message you're trying to convey.

Card 2: The block—This is the thing that is standing in your way. It could be completely internal (for example, like some old stories you tell yourself about how you aren't good enough), or it could be external (for example, fear of judgment).

Card 3: Breakthrough—This card will tell you any specific actions that you need to take to reclaim your authentic self.

Deck Interview Spread

Everything has a vital essence that you can connect to. Your tarot deck is no different! Whether you are just getting to know a new deck or wanting to reconnect with an old favorite, this spread is guaranteed to facilitate communication.

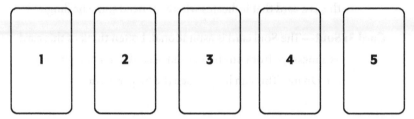

Card 1: Hello!

Card 2: How are we meant to work together?

Card 3: What kind of readings do you love to do?

Card 4: What kind of readings do you not like to do?

Card 5: Any more thoughts?

Creative Support Identification Spread

This is a spread that is intended to help you determine your allies and move forward through difficult times. It sees you in partnership with the tarot to create change in your life. This spread will help you to identify which cards you might want to work with ritualistically over a period of time.

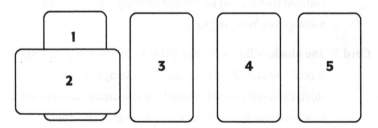

Card 1: What card represents me, in this moment?

Card 2: What card is showing up to support me materially?

Card 3: What card is showing up to be my ally and protector?

Card 4: What card is my teacher?

Card 5: How can I best channel the energy of these cards?

Spreads for Self-Expression

The following spreads are for the creative process and work well from your initial ideas all the way to the completion of a creative project, so feel free to use them at any time in the course of this book.

The Creative Project Energy Analysis

This is a spread that is designed to help you understand the energy of this project and what you bring to it. This is helpful for understanding your relationship to the project. Because your creativity is an important aspect of self-expression, understanding this relationship is essential.

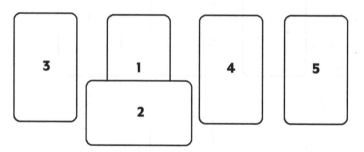

Card 1: The project itself

Card 2: Influences on the project

Card 3: Baggage to leave behind when approaching this project

Card 4: Finding *joy* in the project

Card 5: Next best steps

An Elemental Spread to Aid Your Creative Process

This is a spread that can be done two different ways. You can either separate your cards by suit and then shuffle and lay them out according to their corresponding element *or* you can just do it in a regular style.

The placements are in the order that makes the most sense—each element is placed in its cardinal direction. (Please switch it if that's not true where you're located!) It also makes sense to put these in a straight line, and you can absolutely move it around creatively if it's not working for you.

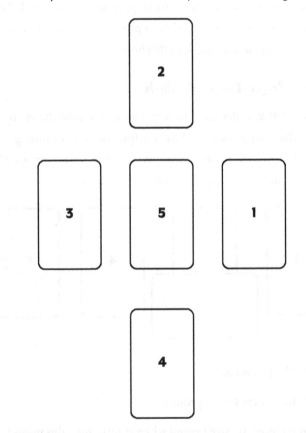

Card 1: Fire—What to do with the initial spark

This is where the cards will help you take an idea or impulse you have and extrapolate on it. Brainstorm away with this card!

Card 2: Air—Where to cut and where to expand

Now we edit the initial idea but remember that early edits also include where we need to expand and give our work more room to fill out.

Card 3: Water—What are you trying to say and why?

This is where the cards help you figure out why *you* are the person to say this on both a personal level and in terms of being a voice for the ideas present in the work.

Card 4: Earth—Where to grow and how to make it last

Alternatively, this placement could be about finalizing it and taking it into the world at large.

Card 5: Spirit—A glimpse at the bigger picture

As a final placement, this shows us where we're headed with the piece. If your creative work is for an audience (it doesn't have to be!) then this shows whom it might end up impacting and what that impact might be on that audience or yourself.

The Six Hats Spread

Coined by Edward de Bono in the book *Six Thinking Hats,* the Six Thinking Hats is a creative thinking concept that involves us imagining putting on six different hats that tap into different parts of our mind/self to help us come up with as many solutions as possible. As soon as we heard about this we knew it was dying to become a tarot spread! The Six Hats are as follows, and the spread is simply laying them out either six in a row or in whatever layout makes sense to you. The colors listed are the ones de Bono uses to explain them and help code the information to make it easier to memorize, so don't worry if you can't connect that to the general information.

While this concept was developed for creative thinking for practical and business solutions, Cassandra uses this spread for a number of different purposes in their work. It can be utilized to play with how your audience will perceive a work, to get into the head of various characters, as general storytelling inspiration, and in overcoming creator's block, just to give a few examples. It also makes sense as a check-in for self-care purposes.

This spread is just laid out in two rows, but feel free to turn that into a straight line, a circle, or whatever else makes sense for you. The final card/hat is where you synthesize and organize the others, so if you want to set that one apart a little bit, you certainly can.

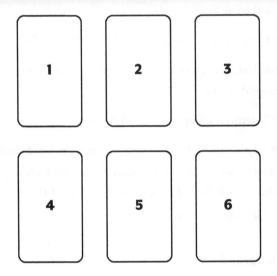

Card 1: White Hat—The facts/emotions/logic part. This side of yourself likes information in concrete, tangible tidbits.

Card 2: Red Hat—Your most emotional self. This is what the inner child and the heart want and what we want when we let our emotions run the show.

Card 3: Black Hat—I sometimes call this the scaredy-cat hat. This is the self that wants us to be cautious, that is suspicious and worried. It's also the hat of discernment, tuning in when we get our messages mixed up.

Card 4: Yellow Hat—This is our most sunny, positive, cheerful self. This is all the naivete of The Fool summated into the most Pollyanna version of ourself we could be.

Card 5: Green Hat—The green hat is the hat concerned with creativity and growth. This hat is the one that pushes us to think outside the box and does not want us to deny or run from our eccentricities.

Card 6: Blue Hat—This is the hat that organizes all these other hats. This side of ourself can see all the other sides and make sense of them and knows how to streamline everything efficiently.

The *Six Thinking Hats* book gets into role play a bit, so if you're feeling adventurous or are a performing artist or actor, allow yourself to role play. Act it out. Really throw yourself into the side of yourself represented by the hat and try to block out noise from any other sides of self that are longing to be heard right now. They'll get their hat in due time.

The Creative Cycle Spread

This spread requires a working knowledge of the Major Arcana; the basic principle is that you lay out twenty-two cards, understanding that the placement for the first one is The Fool, the placement of the second one is The Magician, and so on and so forth until you reach The World. There are three different ways you can do this spread.

If you know the Major Arcana really well you can simply shuffle and lay your cards out.

If you don't know your Majors that well, you can lay them out and use just the Minor Arcana for the spread.

Another option if you're iffy on the Major Arcana is that you can lay out the Majors from one deck and then use a second deck that plays well with the first to lay out the reading itself. This way you have the Majors noted *and* you have a full deck to work with for the reading.

I didn't design a sample illustration because (a) I was afraid it would look messy and not translate in 2D, and (b) I want you to play around with it! Lay them out in logical rows and columns to start but then mix it up! Some story elements may make more sense elsewhere for what you're trying to do, or you can use this as a creative activity simply designed to get you to think about different ideas in different positions.

I've added some potential story prompts/ideas using this spread but your cards might reveal different prompts *or* you might have your own ideas about what each placement should mean based on the Major Arcana card it correlates to.

0   The Fool—The protagonist/central character (place this one above the spread, not in it)

1   The Magician—The first action taken

2   The High Priestess—A hint at what is hidden or what the central character doesn't know yet

3   The Empress—A show of creativity or ingenuity from the central character

4   The Emperor—The central character learning or designing the path ahead

5   The Hierophant—The system in place that the character must adhere to

6   The Lovers—A big choice is made

7   The Chariot—The central character commits to the path ahead

8   Strength—The character's commitment is tested

9   The Hermit—The character finds a spot to rest and consider what their inner voice is saying

10 Wheel of Fortune—An unanticipated change or mix-up

11 Justice—Consequences of the decision in The Lovers are shown

12 The Hanged One—The central character starts seeing things differently

13 Death—The "Act One" end where the character is left with a loss or a door shutting for them

14 Temperance—The character learns to balance who they are now with where they want to go

15 The Devil—Play with a side quest or a night of indulgence to blow off steam for the character

16 The Tower—The big shake-up or the central conflict hitting a head

17 The Star—The character rests and finds their hope is restored

18 The Moon—A dream sequence or an imagining of rewilding

19 The Sun—A celebration as the story wraps up

20 Judgement—The character heads back to where this story started but has clearly changed for the better

21 The World—Some final words from the narrator or denouement

One thing I really like about this spread is that it is so mutable. To personalize it for your own use, think about what each card is saying as part of The Fool's Journey or just as a single card and figure out what that looks like in a story structure for yourself. For example, for The Hermit I could have had the central character meet a Merlin type character, or I could have had them struggle to light a lantern. For The Lovers they could have explored a night of sex and passion with a passerby or found a true companion who would accompany them the rest of the way.

PART TWO

The Major Arcana:
The Inward Journey

6

ARCHETYPES AND SPIRITUAL SELF-CARE

The Major Arcana are life's deepest secrets, personified.

he Major Arcana represent the big, cosmic points in our lives. When these cards come up over and over again in our readings, we know to stop and pay attention. While the Minor Arcana represent keys to the secrets of the everyday world, these cards usher us into a heroic journey. There are so many different angles from which the tarot works for us—it is full of twists and turns. Tarot can be for everyday life, for specific projects, for clients, for big life planning, for dream analysis, and so much more. This is *why* it's such a potent tool for self-care and creative work. The Major Arcana specifically facilitates the creative process, while the Minor Arcana show us *how* we plan to do that work and take care of ourselves.

The Major Arcana helps us understand the backbone of story structure, and it can be really helpful particularly for narrative creators. This part of the tarot is all about larger-than-life archetypes; the Major Arcana represents the flashpoint moments in our life. We always have some kind of Major Arcana energy, moving through the energy of each of these cards as if they are seasons of our life.

. . . .

Styles of witchcraft to play with: Ceremonial magic, casting a Wiccan circle, drawing down the moon, seasonal rites, deep pathworking meditations

. . . .

Styles of creativity to play with: Novel writing, storytelling, character creation, DM-ing a Dungeons and Dragons game

The Major Arcana is organized in a very specific way: *It tells a story.*

Starting with The Fool, and moving through to The World, the Major Arcana unfolds before us. We are The Fool, wandering our way through these new landscapes and meeting new magical allies. We are learning as we go and discovering deeper aspects of ourselves. This wandering journey is often called The Hero's Journey.

Each card of the Major Arcana represents an archetype. Archetypes are a recurrent symbol or motif in literature, art, or mythology. Many occultists and witches work with archetypes as an embodiment of a concept they want to draw into their lives, or as something that will teach them important lessons. Remember that tarot altar-building exercise? That's a part of it. They are also a gateway into understanding how tarot can help us with our creativity.

Tarot uses the language of archetypes to communicate: the archetype is a symbol or motif that we recognize in our unconscious self that speaks to us and therefore helps us read the cards. In the Major Arcana, we see a clear story and we find ourselves in certain places on the journey at specific points in the process.

The structure of the Major Arcana can mirror any type of Hero's Journey. The Hero's Journey is not one thing; it is used in psychology and creative theory to discuss the journey either we or fictional characters make in our lives. There is a huge difference between the psychological hero's journey and the creative hero's journey. Tarot writers often try to bridge the gap, but this book (for obvious reasons) will focus on the creative Hero's Journey.

The Hero's Journey is one tool of many to learn the Major Arcana, but we're using Rachel Pollack's take on it to ease you into this work. Famed tarot expert Pollack noticed that the order of the Major Arcana draws on a heroic story structure, which is why the Majors are often called the Fool's Journey. We meet each of the Major Arcana as if we are The Fool, going through our own story. There's a progression—if the progression weren't important, the Arcana would not be numbered, and that dates back to the very first tarot deck.

The transition from using archetypes as a storytelling technique to their use in magic is fairly natural. In our earlier discussion about tarot and ritual we talked about how the objects and symbols that occultists use represent their intentions playing out in the mundane world. Archetypes themselves can work this way, too. The archetype can become someone that you want to be, an aspect of self that you want to connect with, and it can also represent mentors and teachers in your life.

The Major Arcana then positions us as being in relationship to and also embodying the different archetypes. It helps us to make the connections about what archetypal roles we are playing and perhaps even the figures that we need to seek out. The Major Arcana is a collection of challenges, allies, teachers, and opportunities that are present in our lives. Sometimes we need archetypes that are ultimately supportive—for example, if you are getting married you may want to embody The Lovers to help you make the transition. Sometimes we need the opposite of the energy that we currently have—if we are clinging on to something that isn't working, we might want to embrace the Death card as we get ready for change.

There are so many beautiful archetypes that the popular texts on them don't cover. In Siri's spiritual practice, common archetypes include the Oracle, the Hag, and the Genderbending Trickster. In queer community we both think of archetypes like the community itself, chosen family, Drag Queens, the first brick-thrower at Stonewall, and the incomparable visual archetype of a hot butch in a leather jacket leaning against a brick wall. (That last one just *might* be Cassandra.) Occasionally these *do* make their way into tarot—the *Slow Holler Tarot* actually rewrites The Empress as Kindred, a portrayal we both absolutely love.

Now think about archetypes you love that you haven't seen portrayed often, if at alll. List out some of them. Then journal on what they each mean to you. How do they inspire you to self-care? What self-care do they advise? What do they tell you about self-expression? Where do they lead you or inspire you creatively?

We Are The Fool

This book is structured around The Empress, but there is no way to talk about the Major Arcana without diving deep into The Fool. When we think of the Major Arcana as a journey, it can help us to understand what these massive cards are telling us about this moment in our lives. Are you in a Tower moment or a Star moment? Who is the best ally for you at this time? Are you at the beginning of a phase, or moving toward the end?

Our journey starts with The Fool stepping off a cliff.

When The Fool takes that leap, they are going into unknown waters and opening themselves up for change on a massive scale. They are not sure where they're going, but they are thrilled to be on the road. Each of the Major Arcana that come next are there to teach the Fool something on the way—or perhaps even challenge them.

The Fool from the 1909 Rider-Waite-Smith deck, left, and from *The Radiant Tarot*, 2021, right.

Many people learned tarot working with Rider-Waite-Smith decks, so that's where a lot of their archetypal imagery comes from. In this deck we have a person dressed in a court jester's costume looking up at the sky as they wander their way off a cliff. They have a dog with them, they hold a white rose in one hand, and they balance a bindle on their shoulder. The card itself is very colorful and the person's garb is brightly colored with trailing sleeves. The Fool feels like the most approachable of Smith's illustrations, and they feel like a celebration of tarot itself. As we move through the rest of the cards, we'll explain some of the more esoteric origins for the imagery in this deck and hopefully take these archetypes off a pedestal to create long-term friends for you.

As you begin to work with tarot, it's important to see yourself as a sort of fool. If you work with only one other archetype in the Major Arcana, work with The Fool. It will be so supportive and make this process downright fun. The Fool is a beautiful energy for starting any kind of new endeavor, and they will be a support to you over the years as you continue to start new projects and dive into your creativity.

There are many things you can do to connect with The Fool's energy. There's a curiosity to this card that we (especially as adults) can lose. But that kind of curiosity is important to carry forward, continually, or we lose momentum for growth and change. The same is true for our creative lives. Approaching our work (and play) with a foolish perspective will help us to become truly innovative.

Here are some ways to ritualistically bring The Fool into your life:

- If you keep a spiritual altar, place The Fool card or a printout of a Fool card on your altar.

- Take out The Fool card from your deck. Set it on the table in front of you. Set a timer for 1 minute and do nothing but stare at the card. When the time is up, turn the card over and set a timer for 2 minutes, and try to recount as many details as you can remember about The Fool. At the end of those 2 minutes, flip the card back over and notice what you remembered/forgot.

- Dress up like The Fool on your card! Or perhaps strike their pose! Hold that pose for a certain number of minutes, and see if any feelings come in.

- Place The Fool card in front of you and meditate. You can probably find a guided meditation for The Fool on YouTube, from a tarot content creator, or in a book. You can also record your own meditation to The Fool. A guided meditation is also not necessary.

- Write The Fool a letter! Is there anything you would like to ask them, that perhaps they have learned on their travels? What would you like to learn from The Fool? After you've written your letter, take several deep breaths and start moving your pen across the paper. It might take you a while to get into a trance state, but if you are able, allow your pen to move across the paper and write from the perspective of The Fool.

These are also exercises that you can use with the other cards in the Major Arcana, but The Fool is the gateway. They are the one who will introduce you to the other archetypes as you go.

Who are the characters that The Fool meets on their journey?

The Major Arcana—The Story

Setting The Fool aside, the Major Arcana can be divided into three rows.

The first row of the Major Arcana consists of The Magician through The Chariot, cards 1 through 7. Rachel Pollack describes the first row as *the worldly sequence,* as in learning how the world works. We can also look at the first row as the *ego row,* the row in which The Fool is meeting different aspects of self and getting to know them on a deep level. Each of these archetypes, up until The Chariot, represents different roles that people have in society. The Fool is confronted with the roles that they could potentially fulfill, and they are also asked what roles they want to play. We call it the "ego" row because it is—in our opinion—the most mundane of the rows of the Major Arcana. Of course, The Magician and The High Priestess show us that there is still magic in the mundane.

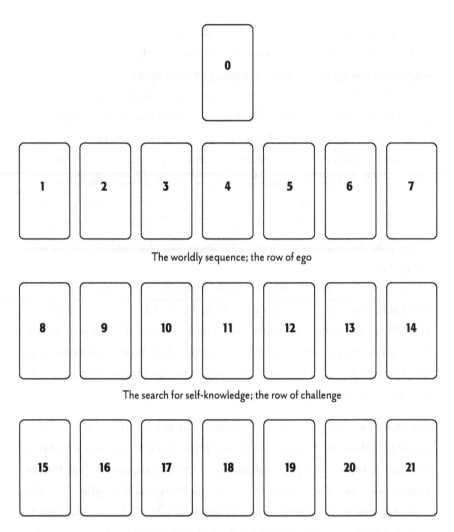

The worldly sequence; the row of ego

The search for self-knowledge; the row of challenge

Enlightenment; the row of change

The Chariot breaks that streak and also allows us to have some momentum moving forward into the next row of the Major Arcana. It is the bridge, the vehicle, the breakthrough.

The second row of the Major Arcana, cards 8 through 14, is called the *row of challenge*, or as Pollack describes it, the "search for self-knowledge." It starts with either Strength or Justice, depending on your deck.[1]

Most decks start their second row with the Strength card, and for simplicity in this book, we will be starting the second row with Strength. This is like bracing ourselves for what is to come. At this point in the Fool's Journey, The Fool is turning toward an inner landscape. They have met figures who are able to help them on the road, but the next thing for them is to define their inner landscape. The Hermit, the Wheel of Fortune, Justice, The Hanged One, Death, and Temperance are all states of being that The Fool cycles through. It is through Strength that the Fool is able to find Temperance.

If the second row of *your* deck starts with Justice, it changes the flow of The Fool's Journey a bit. This means that The Fool is encountering Justice when they turn to their inner knowledge, and this is the thing that they have to carry with them throughout the next row of the Majors. This means that the challenge becomes finding Justice and understanding our own morals as we move through our inner landscape.

The final row of the Major Arcana, cards 15 through 21, is the row of enlightenment, or the *row of change*. We think of this as the cosmic row—the row that moves beyond the personal and back into the collective—but it goes further than that. The cosmic row of the Major Arcana highlights all of the ways that we want to grow beyond our current society. We harness the knowledge that we gained about society in the first row, as well as the lessons we've learned about ourselves from the second row. This row has a lot of steep hills and valleys, ups and downs.

• • •

---

1   This comes down to whether your deck is in the Rider-Waite-Smith, the Thoth, or the Marseilles lineage. When they were creating the deck, Arthur Waite wanted to make the Major Arcana align better with an astrological progression. The Chariot is connected to Cancer, and Strength is associated with Leo. Justice is associated with Libra, but in decks prior to the Rider-Waite-Smith deck, it followed Cancer's card. It made sense to Waite and Smith to change the order of the Major Arcana so that Leo's card would follow Cancer's card.

This three-row narrative structure is the classic Fool's Journey in tarot. In this way of reading the cards, The Fool is meeting people along the way who help them to learn and grow. We are centered as The Fool and often see ourselves in this role, and the lessons we learn are from the perspective of The Fool's Journey. But this book is about learning from The Empress.

So how does The Empress meet each of the cards of the Major Arcana?

Let's now explore that journey.

7

THE EMPRESS'S JOURNEY

Before beginning any journey, The Empress meets **The Fool.** This is a beautiful card of beginning, just taking the leap that you need to take to move forward. When The Empress meets The Fool, the two energies come together to generate new and exciting beginnings. These two are the truly creative powerhouses of the Major Arcana. The Fool brings all of the ideas, and The Empress helps them to choose which ideas to nourish. While the Fool is the one to take the leap, The Empress is there to catch the fall.

The Magician is an outward-facing archetype; they make sure that we have everything we need to move forward on our transformative journey. The Magician is able to use all of the elements to transform into a higher version of themselves. They are able to see that their vision is sacred. *This* is the intersection of The Empress and The Magician. So much of our own work in this book is recognizing that creative work is sacred and that it has the power to transform even beyond our wildest dreams. The Magician is the one who gives The Fool the pep talk; they are responsible for helping The Fool determine their own path forward. The Magician is also a powerful manifestation card—and when paired with The Empress, that manifestation becomes sustainable. When this card comes up, know that you have the power to create something amazing. The stars are aligned to help you see it through to fruition.

Next we meet **The High Priestess,** a different kind of magic worker. This card helps us turn inward to seek transformation. They have a lot of the same magical energy as The Magician, but they focus that energy on learning the inner mysteries. They have access to the Great Unknown of the occult and will reveal their secrets only when the time is right. The High Priestess upholds the idea of mysteries, understanding that sometimes secrets are necessary to protect our wisdom. The High Priestess is also deeply concerned with intuition. While The Magician is here to help us with manifesting our desires in the real world, The High Priestess wants us to connect with our intuition to find our way forward and to learn what is in our highest and best good. When The Empress meets The High Priestess, they are welcomed beyond the veil of everyday reality and into another plane of existence. The High Priestess is the threshold into our inner realms. The Empress then turns around and helps us to express those inner realms, but only after we truly get to know ourselves.

Next comes the card that is the focus of our book—**The Empress** themself. When The Empress meets theirself, they are overflowing with ideas, follow-through, and abundance. They nurture themselves and are able to carry things forward because of the time they take to rest and recuperate. The Empress is at home in themself, and that feeling of home within is where abundance, joy, and unconditional nurturance come from. This is an important skill that we must learn early and utilize often. That's why this archetype shows up so early in the Major Arcana; this is one of the building blocks of the entire creative and self-defining process that is the Major Arcana.

After The Empress, we meet **The Emperor.** They represent the government and authority, and this archetype can be very harsh. As we talked about in the intro, both Cassandra and Siri are committed to breaking gender stereotypes with the cards. The Empress and The Emperor are an obvious and very important pairing, though they do not have to exist on opposite ends of a binary. We have already extensively rewritten The Empress as being about nurturing and creativity—femininity can be a part of that, but people of all gender identities and expressions can access Empress energy. When thinking about The Emperor in partnership with The Empress, it's easier to get past the austere and foreboding imagery when we divorce them from toxic masculinity. The Emperor wants you to thrive just as much as The Empress does—but they express it through creating systems, structures, and rules. The Emperor is also an incredibly important card as it relates to leadership. When The Fool meets The Emperor, they are learning about how to rule and how rulership works in the outside world. In terms of creativity, the Emperor can help us to find the discipline needed to follow through on creative projects.

The Hierophant can be another difficult archetype to work with, particularly because *hierophant* is a bit of an outdated word. The *Oxford English Dictionary* defines a hierophant as "a person, especially a priest in ancient Greece, who interprets sacred mysteries or esoteric principles." Very often, the Hierophant stands in as an archetype of traditional religion. In the Rider-Waite-Smith deck, the Hierophant looks like the Pope. A lot of other decks have reimagined this archetype as a sort of messenger or intermediary between spiritual and the mundane. It's a different kind of intuition than the High Priestess exhibits. This is a lot more about a combination of message and power, and conventional methodologies. In terms of our creative life, this is how we can learn from traditional outlooks on our medium. Perhaps it is joining an artist or trade guild or reading classics. The Hierophant and The Empress bring inspiration and research together, showing how opposite personalities can come together for a shared goal.

Connection is the theme of our next card. **The Lovers** is one of those cards that is so sweet when we meet them that they seem obvious in their meanings. Of course, The Lovers card represents love and commitment to love. In our creative lives, this is one of the reasons we create; it is the joy that we receive from the creative process. The Lovers also represent a sort of divine connection to our work—we see this from the angel that so often unites the lovers. This card teaches us about relating to another person when you love them so deeply, when you want to be a true partner with them. Until now, there hasn't really been a card with multiple people on equal footing, so this is all about the relational sphere. This is essential, as the first few cards of the

Major Arcana are all about The Fool exploring different societal roles and how they should be played out. Many tarot readers see this card as representative of choice. This can also represent The Empress realizing they need to make choices in relation to how those choices impact their loved ones.

The Chariot rounds out the first row of the Major Arcana. The Chariot represents breaking through, understanding what you want to do, and going for it. This is an important time for us because The Chariot represents clarity of what we really want to do. When The Empress meets The Chariot, they clarify their direction and a motive. The Chariot can also represent a moment of pause to reflect and determine if you are really on the path that you want to go on. With the energy of The Chariot, you can change direction. This is a moment when the words are flowing, when you are feeling a sort of divine inspiration. The Chariot can also represent the end of a creative block and charging forward. What would The Chariot look like with The Empress at the helm?

For the sake of simplicity in this book, we will start this second row with the **Strength** card. Strength is the need to fortify yourself to move into these more shadowy realms of the Major Arcana. The Strength card is often about balancing force and compassion. It is taming the lion. In many cases, that lion can end up being an overcharged ego. Taming it can help us to move deeper into our work and life. Another word for strength is fortitude—gathering the means necessary to continue on. The Strength card becomes the fortitude necessary to journey into our shadows and to explore our inner self in new and startling ways. The Empress works with Strength to have the courage necessary to express themself. This does take courage for a lot of people—and the reward is sweet.

Right after encountering and gathering our Strength, we meet **The Hermit**. Sometimes this is a card of literal solitude, but more often than not it is a card of mentorship and study. The Hermit is like that wise person we meet in the forest who can help us train for the next leg of the journey. The Hermit is often depicted carrying a lantern, which represents the inner knowledge and wisdom they offer. We can draw on this spark for our own creative spirit, the gift of The Hermit. This card can also help us when we are at a point of needing to expand our knowledge and learn from a mentor about the technical aspects of our work. The Hermit is essential for any kind of teaching and mentorship role. They can be a guide in dark times when we need to access new and startling visions. When The Empress and The Hermit work together, it means coming to a gentle understanding of how our work impacts our personal development.

If The Hermit is a very slow energy, the **Wheel of Fortune** is a fast one that throws us forward. The Wheel of Fortune is of course related to luck, prosperity, and destiny, but it's more than that. The Wheel of Fortune is a sense of something larger than we can comprehend. When this wheel comes hurtling into our lives, it is likely that there is an idea or spark that is necessary for us to follow. This shows us when we have the support of the energy of the moment, when our work is likely to get in front of the people who need to see it the most. Within the Wheel of Fortune is also a balance of elements and the whole mystery school of the tarot. In general, whenever this card comes up it's important to surrender to the moment. Attempting to control fortune or fate will not turn out well for you—but it is also important to recognize that you don't need to control fortune at this moment. It is already in your favor, so go with the flow.

Moving on from the Wheel of Fortune we have **Justice**. Justice is finding that balance in our work, tapping into some kind of eternal Truth that needs to pour out. The challenge of the Justice card is in putting our ideals into our creative work. This can make us feel very vulnerable, and it can even be alienating if you don't have a strong support system that shares your values. On the other hand, when the Justice energy is not strong in your work, you could feel isolated from it, or as if it doesn't matter. Of course your work matters—your voice matters. But the Justice card challenges you to align that voice with something greater, to look around at your community and see where your voice is needed. None of us creates in a vacuum, and this is an indication of where your creative work is in conversation with greater social justice movements. The Empress is concerned with ideas of fairness and equity, and in this way they have a kinship with the figure on the Justice card.

The Hanged One represents suspension, waiting, a slow energy of surrender. Traditionally, this card represents self-sacrifice, especially for a greater cause. The Hanged One is most often suspended from one leg, upside down, getting a new perspective on things. When you are in a Hanged One period of your life you might feel like you spend a lot of time waiting but at the very end of this period you will have a huge revelation. That is what The Hanged One teaches The Empress—patience and trust in the process even if it's difficult. In your creative life, The Hanged One might show up as a creative block. We also like to think of this as a time to look for creative input, rather than simply creative output. We need to take in new ideas and art forms in order to be inspired, and so if you are feeling blocked, surrender to that block. Seek new perspectives and perhaps begin creating in a very different medium. This is a signal that you aren't in a time of production, but rather rest and regeneration. Remember all of the ways that The Empress invites you into rest.

After The Hanged One comes **Death**. Often this is a metaphorical death and less a physical one. The Death card helps us to shed our skin and reemerge. Change is one of the greatest challenges in life, and the tarot is here to help us weather it. Even necessary changes are hard and sometimes require the ending of something we loved. The Death card shows up most often for me when there is a massive change that I need to surrender to, but that I am absolutely avoiding. It's not pretty. You might be tempted to hear that the Death card represents change and dismiss the naturally difficult aspects of Death. However, this is not to sugarcoat this difficult card. You could experience the death and change of something that is really important to you. Death often ushers in a phase of grief. Thankfully, we have already experienced surrender in the Hanged One, but surrendering to the grief process can be difficult. Give yourself whatever space you need to grieve things as they were and to move into something new and beautiful. The Empress experiences Death as much as any of us do—projects that are doomed, ideas or hobbies that get ruined for you, perhaps even the death of an important mentor or inspiration. Take time to grieve.

Temperance is the last card of the second row of the Major Arcana. This is a built-in space to process the grief of the Death card. One of my very favorite queer decks (*Slow Holler Tarot*) renames this card as The Alchemist, and I find that so fitting for Temperance energy. Temperance is a card of rest, yes, but it is also a card of integrating the difficult lessons you've learned so far. This often leads to a transformation from one state into another—an alchemical transcendence. It is time to make choices based on the challenges you have been given during this row of the Major Arcana. The Temperance card is all about transforming and transmuting those challenges, bringing power to them. Sometimes the Temperance card signals that it's time for us to rest, and sometimes it signals that it's time for us to get moving. Rather than being a card of pure rest, it is a card of balance. Thinking about it that way, we can apply this to our creative work through knowing that there is a time when we are in creative flow, and also knowing that there might be a time when we need to take a step back because we've been overextending ourselves. Both of these are necessary for our creative work. The Empress may have a tendency toward overconsumption, and this is one of the lessons The Empress needs to learn.

The Devil calls us into the third row of the Major Arcana. Traditionally, The Devil is a hard card—mirroring a lot of our bad habits and self-destructive tendencies. However, we read this card as a liberator, a breaker of chains, a fallen angel who dared to stand up to God. The Devil is a defiant archetype who asks us what we want. There are no limits with The Devil, which can be its own challenge—particularly if you struggle with overindulgence and substance abuse issues. We choose to see The Devil as a liberator, as one who is willing to be defiant where it is necessary to be defiant. This is the first hurdle to cross in changing the world fundamentally. In terms of our creative lives, The Devil has so many applications. That project that doesn't "fit" with what you've got going on? The Devil wants you to give in. Those old habits or negative self-talk that are contributing to a complete creative block? The Devil shows you these, so that you can overcome them. When The Empress meets The Devil, there is an embarrassment of riches: treating yourself to lavish dinners, your favorite expensive perfume, and indulgent nights on the town.

After the Devil comes one of the most feared cards in the tarot: **The Tower**. The Tower is not just a break from the past, but absolute destruction of the way things were. This often feels painful. If you haven't let go of the things that you need to let go, The Tower comes in to force your hand. This is a card of extremely harsh truth, and it is also the card of destruction. When you have built a fortress to a false ideal, when there are things that are absolutely not working in your life, The Tower is there to break you free from them—or else. The third row of the Major Arcana represents the shattering of consciousness and ego. It is only after letting go of these things that we are able to begin anew and create something better. Speaking creatively, The Tower can mean that projects blow up in our face, or we are forced to start from scratch when our assumptions about our work are shattered. When Cassandra references subtracting Judgment of Self in order to hit a true creative surge, this is work often done in or made possible because of The Tower. The Empress learns from this card that the things we refused to let die naturally in The Death card will come to their end in a much more dramatic way in The Tower.

The great destruction of The Tower leaves behind a bit of a wasteland but it's where we begin moving to creativity proper. **The Star** is here to help us pick up the pieces, to give us a chance to rest and catch our breath. This is the dream that emerges once we are finally able to sleep. Very often, The Star is described as a visionary who rises from the rubble. And we think it's important to see that vision as hard-won. Another extremely important lesson of The Star is to take your time and allow yourself to rest when you have made it to the other side of a major upheaval. This is another place where we think it's important to think about creative inputs. We really, truly need to feed the artist within, especially when we've been through a traumatic shake-up. Take a trip to a museum, read a favorite book, listen to inspiring playlists; all of these can help to awaken the inner Star. The other thing that is so very visionary about The Star is that they are able to produce something that is totally new and do it from a place of rest and healing. This is where The Empress innovates; we have destroyed convention and are able to create something foreign and healing.

The Moon is one of the last cards that we think of as being a part of the unconscious realm of the tarot. The next card, The Sun, feels like a return of sorts to the "everyday world." But for now, we are still in the shadowy realm of the unknown. This card helps us do several things: tap into our unconscious and intuitive selves, create new cycles and patterns outside of patriarchy, and also make peace with the unknown. The Moon's medicine is that we don't actually need to have all the answers or know everything right away. Hanging out in the liminal cosmic space that The Star and The Moon comprise is counter to so many of the lessons that we are taught. What does it feel like not to have a direction? How can you trust yourself while you discover your direction? The Moon reminds The Empress that creativity has cycles, that there is a wax and wane to our work. The Moon allows The Empress to get even weirder. We're building the confidence to bring the bizarre aspects of our creativity to the public.

The Sun is a breakthrough moment. After all of this time shut away in our own process, the Sun is when we're finally able to let ourselves be seen. At this point, The Fool has been through a deeply personal journey into the depths of their own psyche, and The Sun represents bringing all of that wisdom out. In the Rider-Waite-Smith deck, The Sun card shows a naked child riding a horse away from a walled garden. This is the reemergence of the Self, born again and new. The Sun card can also be a symbol of Beginner's Mind. This is a concept in Zen Buddhism that basically represents having an attitude of openness, eagerness, and a lack of preconceptions when approaching something new.[2] Throughout our journey, perceptions have been shattered over and over again, and in this way The Empress reemerges with the wisdom and tools necessary to approach everything with a lack of judgment. This does not mean a lack of wisdom or discernment, but rather an openness to begin

---

2   If you would like more information on Beginner's Mind, I recommend *Zen Mind, Beginner's Mind* by Shunryu Suzuki.

anew. In terms of creativity, this is the beginner's mind necessary to constantly approach our work with fresh eyes, to allow ourselves to play around and experiment. The Sun is an allowance, permission to be yourself in all of your glory.

Judgment is the penultimate card in the Major Arcana, and it can feel like a harsh awakening after The Sun. After being in such a happy, blissful, unstructured place, Judgment can feel particularly difficult to grapple with. However, this is necessary as the story of the Majors comes to a close. Judgment is the final integration of the lessons that you've learned along the way. In this card, we are brought before a higher force and asked what we have learned. This is the point in the movie where the protagonist faces a situation that they have learned to deal with, that would have sent them spiraling at the beginning of the story. Think about in *Labyrinth* when Sarah faces the goblin king and says, "You have no power over me." That moment is powerful because she can repeat the line she kept forgetting at the beginning—she has also literally found her power on the journey. That is the essence of this card: learning your power, standing in it, and integrating all of the wisdom you've learned along the way. The Empress and Judgment together help you to understand how to express these ideals and how to learn from your past mistakes. The Empress softens the accountability of Judgment so that it's easier to understand.

Finally, we come to **The World**. The World contains everything. It is the card that represents the ultimate enlightenment of the tarot, and at the same time it is the card that transcends all of that. Just as The Fool contains all possibility, The World contains an abundance of riches. Whenever this card shows up, know that there is a cycle that is coming to an end. Not just any end—but a satisfying end. It's almost difficult to even talk about The World card because of how very much it carries. This is the flourish of creativity, when your project is out in the world, and you are able to take a break and rest. This is finally performing that play that you have been working on for months. This is the moment of seeing your book on the shelf at bookstores. This is an incredible moment of reclamation and completion. You've earned it.

Numerologically, The World (21) connects right back to The Empress (3). Of course it does. The World, like The Empress, is a card that begs the senses to come alive, asks us to pay attention to our environment, and pushes us to move forward in the world confidently. When we look at The World in this way, as the conclusion of the journey of the Major Arcana as well as our own creative process, we know what The Empress is trying to teach us. The World isn't just about endings. It's *satisfactory* endings. It's the rush of pride during applause at a show opening. It's getting positive reviews of your latest book. It's all of the things that remind us that self-care is also community care. That creativity encourages connection. That learning from and pathworking with The Empress opens up whole new Worlds for you.

• • •

When we look at the Major Arcana through the lens of what lessons The Empress is trying to teach us, we see plenty of opportunity for imagination, for reflection, for expression, and of course for release of Judgment of Self. That latter lesson leads us to a freedom that many tarot books try to work us toward in their Major Arcana sections, and The Empress is happy to push us that way, reminding us we are regal. Ultimately we end in The World. Synthesis. Completion. Freedom. Creativity.

Keywords for the Major Arcana

As we walk you through each suit, we want to leave space for you to take everything we've talked about, including and especially your own understanding of things like archetypes and the Hero's Journey, and pair some quick keywords with them. For the traditional meanings, we could have also said "popular" or "common" meanings—we know each tradition is different, but this references how most tarot writers categorize the cards. This means we've included keywords we personally do not work with that often, so feel free to react to them in your own keywords.

Card	Traditional Meanings	Personal Interpretations
0 The Fool	Beginnings Innocence Clear conscience The Hero	
1 The Magician	Magic Power Construction Creation	
2 The High Priestess	Intuition Clairvoyance Premonition Perceptivity	
3 The Empress	Femininity Creativity Abundance	
4 The Emperor	Masculinity Authority Government	
5 The Hierophant	Tradition (especially traditional spirituality) Conventionalism Institutionalism	
6 The Lovers	Partnership Passion Love Commitment	
7 The Chariot	Victory Control Jurisdiction Breaking through barriers	

Card	Traditional Meanings	Personal Interpretations
8 Strength	Fortitude Security Compassion Force	
9 The Hermit	Wisdom Solitude Learning Erudition	
10 Wheel of Fortune	Kismet Destiny Serendipity Luck	
11 Justice	Justice Equilibrium Fairness Equality	
12 The Hanged One	Self-sacrifice Suspension Prophesy Grace	
13 Death	Transformation Mortality Suffering Change	
14 Temperance	Balance Alchemy Harmonization Attunement	
15 The Devil	Bondage Temptation Seduction Addiction	

Card	Traditional Meanings	Personal Interpretations
16 The Tower	Hubris Sudden fall Destruction Faulty foundations	
17 The Star	Hope Optimism Visionary Inspiration	
18 The Moon	Reflection Changes Imagination Cycles	
19 The Sun	Attainment Glory Majesty Celebrity	
20 Judgment	Awakening Epiphany Spiritual realization Judgment	
21 The World	Fulfillment Completion Masterpiece	

Sometimes it's helpful to actually see the three rows of the Major Arcana and learn the Fool's Journey that way. Lay out your own deck's Major Arcana this way, with The Fool set aside and the three rows right on top of each other. We'll use the Rider-Waite-Smith deck here since it's familiar to most people.

Look at the first row. What do you notice about this story?

Look at the second row. What do you notice about this story?

Look at the third row. What do you notice about this story?

Now look down the columns. The columns show a sort of evolution in the Major Arcana. What do you see from this exercise? Analyze the columns below:

Magician—Strength—The Devil

The High Priestess—The Hermit—The Tower

The Empress—Wheel of Fortune—The Star

The Emperor—Justice—The Moon

The Hierophant—The Hanged One—The Sun

The Lovers—Death—Judgment

The Chariot—Temperance—The World

. . . .

What have you learned about the story of the Major Arcana? How would you tell this story?

How do these cards build off of one another?

What card of the Major Arcana do you feel most connected to right now? Why? What card would you *like* to feel most connected to?

. . . .

Major Arcana Spreads

Three Rows of the Major Arcana Spread

Separate out the Major Arcana cards from your deck, and then separate them into the three rows of the Major Arcana. Keep The Fool separate—it will act as a representation of you in the spread.

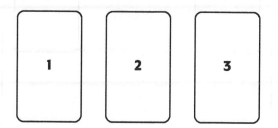

Shuffle the three stacks of cards and choose one for each row:

Card 1: Who is my best role model at this time?

Card 2: What self-knowledge do I need to cultivate at this time?

Card 3: At what stage of change am I?

The Narrative Spirit Spread

You can think of this as a spread to analyze a part of your life and the direction you want to go, or you could use it to help get in touch with the project you are working on. This spread follows the different cycles in Dan Harmon's Plot Embryo to help you figure out where you are now and where the story will go.

Card 1: You, now—This is the "normal," or before, part of the story. For example: character introductions. You or your main characters are in a zone of comfort.

Card 2: Need—You or your protagonist is dissatisfied and wants some kind of change. This could also be a need that is enforced on the character.

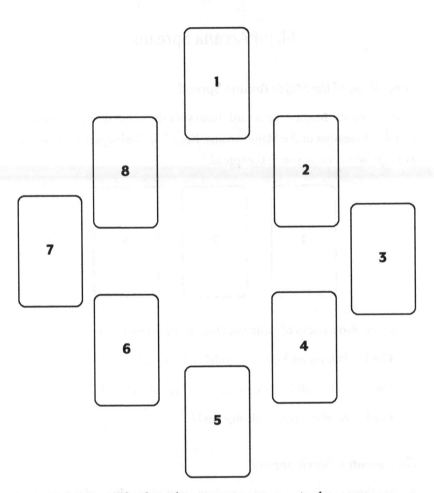

Card 3: Go—The thing that gets you or your main character to move ahead.

Card 4: Search—The hardships your protagonist faces as they move through the story. This is often a really difficult time for the character; think cleansing by fire.

Card 5: Find—The protagonist gets what they wanted, but it might look different than they thought it would. This is where the character needs to make a decision.

Card 6: Take—After finding what they seek, the protagonist takes it. They may need to sacrifice something great for it.

Card 7: Return—The protagonist begins the long journey home.

Card 8: Change—The protagonist has changed, for better or worse. This is often the point of wrapping up the major themes of your work.

Major Arcana Activities

Major Arcana Self-Care Prompts

1. **Look through the Major Arcana and pull out a card or two that really resonate with you right now.** Grab your journal and make some notes about the first things that jump out at you. Are you excited about these cards, or is there some hesitancy? What symbols seem most important to you? What colors are you drawn to? Now think about ways that those symbols might be encouraging you to rest or to treat yourself.

2. **Build an altar to The Lovers.** Put items on it that remind you to take care of yourself. This could be a piece of rose quartz, your favorite scented candle, a bottle of perfume, anything that feels decadent and loving. Check in with this altar any time you are feeling self-critical.

Major Arcana Creative Prompts

1. **Make a list of all of your favorite movies that use the concepts of archetypes** (for example, *The Dark Crystal*, *The NeverEnding Story*). Watch them again and take notes. Which of the archetypes do you find the most appealing?

2. **Go on a physical journey!** I find that sometimes the very act of travel helps to get me into a liminal headspace. This can also just be taking a different bus route than you normally take or going for a long drive. See what happens and if it shifts your perspective.

3. **Find other stories.** We explored the Major Arcana through the Fool's Journey concept, but there are tons of other stories within these cards. Lay your Majors out and see what story, story structure, or ideas you come up with that deviate from that. Move cards around or tell a different tale altogether.

Major Arcana and Creative Magic

The Major Arcana are heavy-hitting cards, and they blend into spellwork really nicely. Working with Major Arcana cards is a powerful way to call in specific energy, either as a spirit aid to your working or as an energy to consciously embody. When you're working with the card as a spirit, you'll need to think about the figures on the card and create them in your mind. You can call them into meditation and ask for their help. For example, if you are having trouble recognizing yourself as regal, or deserving of nourishment, you could place The Empress card on your altar and call on their energy. Then you can ask for their blessing or ask them to help you see yourself as regal.

Spell: Spark Ideas with The Fool

This spell is to help you generate new ideas when you're feeling stuck. This could be a thorny issue in your creative work, or a full-on creative block. The most important thing is to approach this spell with openness and curiosity. This spell was inspired by Rachael Stephens's Bright Ideas Spell, but Siri adapted it to charm an aspect of your space to enhance creativity. After all, our spaces are a huge part of our inspiration!

Materials:

- The Fool card from your tarot deck

- A feather

- A light bulb (the light bulb from your desk lamp/main work space is a great option!)

- Any materials that remind you of the project you're working on, or that evoke creativity more generally to you

Step One: Identify which ideas you would like to spark. Again, this can be related to a specific project or to spark ideas more broadly.

Step Two: Gather all materials and lay them out. Lay The Fool in front of you, and stare at the card. Really stare. Think about The Fool as if they are with you; feel your energy connecting with the energy of The Fool.

Step Three: Pick up the light bulb. Think about how it feels when you have ideas flowing, how you want to feel at your most creative. Imagine that energy is pushing through your hands and into the light bulb. When you feel that it has connected to the light bulb, put it down and clap or snap three times.

Do the same with any objects for your specific project but think about how it feels to work on that specific project.

Step Four: Screw the light bulb into your lamp. Whenever you turn on that specific light bulb and sit down to do some creative work, it will help you have more ideas.

PART THREE

The Minor Arcana: The Journey to Self-Acceptance

8

WANDS–FROM SPARK TO FINISH

The themes of the suit of Wands include:
Gut Instinct, Passion, Excitement, Action, and Raw Creativity.

Each segment of the tarot deck is broken down into smaller narratives (a.k.a. stories). We just journeyed through the story of the Major Arcana. In the same way, each suit tells its own unique stories based on their overall theme.

The Wands don't end as happily as some of the other suits, so we're going to explore the Wands as a lesson in and an example of what happens when we don't nourish or temper our flames. As a story structure, this will most likely fit the idea of a fable. In the case of the journey through the Wands, we're following a cute, fiery fable—then we're hit with the lesson at the end, when it all falls apart.

Our story in our journey through the suit of Wands will deviate at times from the straightforward fable because we'll touch on how our inner fire can be expressed creatively even under duress, and we'll explore what happens when we *do* follow that muse and listen to our flame when it needs to be nourished or tempered and the project simply ends. We want to show the beautiful side of these flames and what happens when it all goes right—but to do that, the Wands do show us hard lessons, too.

The suit of Wands connects to the element of Fire. Fire and Wands both speak to our gut instinct, our passions, excitement, action, potential, sex, and other carnal desires. In a ritual the Wand is what conducts the energy of the magic, so Wands also represent our internal power. For our purposes, the Wands also speak to raw creativity itself. We begin a creative process because there is a primal desire and need to do so. There is a piece of us that comes up with ideas easily and drives us to the things that inspire and empower us. Wands correlate directly to those pieces of ourselves.

As raw, primal creativity Wands also speak to any time we feel struck by inspiration and need to just *Get. It. Out.* This is the part that connects to the muse even if the muse itself is best represented by the Majors or Cups. When Siri and I had the idea to reimagine this book out of course materials, that was our Wands self speaking to us. As we go on in our literary lives making more books and our witchy lives creating more classes, it'll be Wands energy attracting us to the projects we are working on.

As we develop our artistic practices and disciplines, the Wands also speak to the creative outlets we are passionate about. Cassandra wakes up in the morning thinking about books and theatre, and that's their own Wands side coming out. They feel "on fire" after seeing a really well-done movie, and that's Wands energy, too. As we become more aware of how creative works fill out the world around us, the Wands show us which parts we are most drawn to, and the Wands keep us coming back to root and find a home in them.

Inspiration alone isn't enough for the audacious Wands cards though—they are also the drive to take action and they are action itself. While they are the spark that ignites our ability to create, they are also the part of us that jumps into action. The Wands are the suit we identify with as activists and those looking to create a better world, and it is certainly one of the suits best suited for creators of any kind to connect with. While the Pentacles might represent your audience or material, the Swords your thought process or communication, the Cups the creative work itself and your right to self-expression, the Wands are the *imagination* (and motivation) driving us forward.

The downside to the Wands is that fire alone cannot sustain us. If not fed and nourished, a fire burns out on its own. The candle ends, and you need to light a new one. On the flip side, without boundaries, Wands become like a wildfire destroying anything in its path. It takes feeding our creative fire to keep the fire going, and it takes knowing when to call it quits to keep us healthy. Because fire is so boundless and has a mind of its own, follow-through is an issue. Know that this suit will get the ball rolling for you, but you'll likely need to find a way to see a project through elsewhere.

. . . .

Styles of witchcraft to play with: candle magic; spells that call for burning things; anything with gut instinct; any kitchen witchery with intense heat, spices, or both; yoga that zeroes in on kundalini or abdomen; releasing magic; sun magic; sex magic.

. . . .

. . . .

Styles of creativity to play with: anything physical (dancing, drag, movement-based theatre, and the like), cooking or baking, especially over a hot stove or fire, charcoal drawing, anything you are instinctively good at, freestyle writing, impassioned music like hip-hop and rock, pottery and sculpture that has to go in the kiln, erotica.

. . . .

. . . .

Notable other tarot cards featuring Wands: The Magician, The Emperor, The Chariot, The Hermit

. . . .

The Journey through the Wands

As we navigate the suits of the Minor Arcana, you'll see different examples of story and story structure. You can play with these in your own cards (and look for more). The story Cassandra is telling here is rooted in the structure of fables to differentiate it from the Hero's Journey of the Major Arcana.

The Wands in general are catalysts to action, divinity, and creation. They represent our raw creative energy and our drive to do something with that. The Ace is all of that raw potential boiled down into a single card. The **Ace of Wands** is ready to inspire you and unlock all of the beautiful, creative recesses of your body and mind. Spiritually this card is the cosmic spark—as a metaphor that means we're taking the spark inside of us that all creation comes from and watching it blaze brightly, grabbing the torch when we are ready, and doing brilliant things with it. More tangibly, this card is the moment we decide to throw ourselves into a passion project or carnal pleasures for self-care. It is those moments we feel the muse speaking to us clear as crystal for creative purposes.

The Ace sets our hearts on fire and allows us to come up with ideas for creating. In the **Two of Wands**, we take that and turn it into something real. We're still letting our imaginations run a little bit wild but we're trying to formulate a plan. We're taking all of that passion and potential, and we're acting on it. This might mean gathering our ideas and materials into a single place or making an outline or a storyboard of what we want to do while still giving ourselves grace to discover new things along the way. If our fire is going to go out, we still don't have any major signs of that yet. If we have just enough energy to keep this project going, then this card represents the healthiest version of that, where we are using the planning stage not only to storyboard, think the project through, and gather our materials but also to put contingency plans in place in case we start to go overboard or get too tired for the work to be good.

The **Three of Wands** takes that energy of the Two and expands on it. The Three wants us to look for opportunities we haven't explored yet and keep shaping our ideas into a solid plan. We can also begin creating based on our storyboard or outline here and allow that to take us wherever it needs to. I often see this card as a fairly wanderlusty one, where we're not super happy where we are. I actually think this is a really standard place for artists to sit when the planning is more or less done but we're not diving into the work we want to be doing yet. I do suggest, if you also feel a restlessness in this card, that you do start your creative work as you're tidying up your plans. That restlessness is your gut, your soul, your fire wanting to create and if we're going to avoid a big blowup, it's important to feed that now.

Threes in the tarot correlate back to The Empress themself. If this is a card of expansion, that shows us that The Empress wants us to want more for ourselves. If this card is about unexplored opportunities, then we know that The Empress doesn't want us to miss out on anything. As creatively fired as the Wands cards are, this Three really leans into the pleasure principle that The Empress holds so precious. Creativity and imagination become a catalyst for exploring life and pushing bounds here, ensuring that whatever life has to offer—we're not gonna miss our chance to be a part of it.

As we approach the **Four of Wands**, we're feeling really good about our ideas and what they're shaping into. We maybe even finish a rough draft or share what we're working on with others. We take advantage of the opportunities that arise in the Three, and we take a few moments to celebrate how far we've come. This card is commonly seen as one of moving physical homes and is even more commonly seen as the metaphor of that. Fours in numerology and tarot numerology (which can and do have some differences) often represent a period of reevaluation. Reevaluation is a great act of self-care because we are asking not only if something is still working, but also if we are still happy. The Four of Wands trusts that if the answer to that question is "no," you will be able to move forward to something happier and more celebratory.

In the Four of Wands, we want to look at where we are as we are enlivened with divine creative spark and reevaluate the original plans we set. As we reevaluate, we are both fine-tuning our work and reconsidering why we are actually doing this piece. When I reviewed art professionally, I looked for "why is this person/group of people creating this piece at this time?" If that wasn't clear the work itself was usually muddy. Your work can absolutely be good if you're just doing it because you want to—but it should be clear in every facet of the work that it is a passion project, and that that passion is why you're doing it. The Four of Wands simply asks us to make sure that's clear, and that is perhaps what needs to be reevaluated. As a card of movement, this card also asks us to think about where we want this project to end up. Again, there are no wrong answers. Yet a plan isn't truly formulated until you know how to get from the impetus in cards 1 to 3 to the finishing of it.

However, when we dive in to get back to work on our creations with fresh eyes in the **Five of Wands**, we struggle a bit. This card of conflict shows where things maybe aren't as cohesive as we thought, or else it highlights where our vision doesn't quite match up to what's needed practically. While this is a low-energy card in terms of stamina, it'll likely plant some seeds of doubt that we'll continue to struggle with. Some of that may be perceived creative competition with others, and often this card comes up because we've been spending too much time focusing on what other people are doing. It's a reminder not to get buried in how we're being perceived or how *successful* our piece may be while we're still in the creative stage. This is critical in the creative process but more importantly, it's vital for self-care. Without walking away from drama and conflict that doesn't serve you, the Five of Wands shows up to warn you that things are going to get messy and untenable fast, both for your emotional state and probably for your art as well.

In the immediate, we're able to get on top of it. The **Six of Wands** shows victory, triumph, and success. We continue on our path toward following our inspiration, and we are extremely satisfied with what comes from that. I also think of this card as a creative boost when we're talking about creativity and creating. The Five can drain our energy and make us wonder why we're even doing this. This is a natural stage of the process though and it quickly gives way to this Six, which throws us back into the game both in terms of putting paint to canvas and in feeling connected to what you're creating.

From there we go proudly into the **Seven of Wands** where we are able to defend our creation and our point of view in creating it. What does that mean for us when we're talking about our creative work? It's easy to say the work itself should defend its own point of view, but it's your name going on the piece. Are you going to be happy with it as is? Sometimes these more challenging cards refer to our internal conflicts, which we saw in the Five of Wands. We revisit the idea of watering down or overloading our work here. We likely need to make some crucial edits so we can actually be confident letting the work stand on its own.

Other keywords and interpretations for this card include protection and perseverance. In the creative process itself, we come to this point in the story and our fire has already started flickering out. It's really important now to figure out what our spark needs. What makes us feel driven? What makes us feel ready to go back in even when it's tedious? This card asks you to call on these things and, again, trust our drive and our voice when it does come back.

The **Eight of Wands** is all swiftness and fast action. After the Seven, we may have felt like the wind was quickly draining from our sails but the Eight screams in, providing a needed overflow of ideas and opportunities. When it comes to a lot of things in life, this can be a mixed message. It's a lot of things happening at once. At our day jobs, that's probably not great. Our creative lives are different though. Fire isn't meant to sustain and divine inspiration is meant to flow from our mouths, fingers, or bodies and then settle onto the materials we're using. It's good, especially after that seven, that our spark and creativity are swirling around us. They've become hard to get a grip on, but that's precisely what creating is for. You learned how to edit earlier in the suit, so it's okay to let it pour out knowing you'll fix it later.

As we move into the **Nine of Wands,** we are able to set some boundaries and get the grip that we worried about in the Eight. It's hard, but we're able to do it. We see all of that fire, all of that combination action and idea flourish for a moment. We're getting weary, but we know this sprint is almost over and we're able to take a deep breath and regroup. We are able to put the finishing touches on for now, but we are a bit worse for wear. If our creative process has included nourishment and tempering, this is nothing to worry about. We're almost done, and soon we'll be able to breathe easier so it's doable to fling ourselves into these final touches. If we've gone off track, given too much, or gotten totally bogged down in the process, however, we will see ourselves collapse and perhaps even be unable to finish soon.

Finally, we get to the Ten. The **Ten of Wands** is one of the harder cards in the tarot for a lot of people. This is a card where we are burnt out and can't imagine doing one more thing. This card is likely showing up in your creative process because you didn't heed the warnings of earlier cards to give in to self-care and take longer breaks *or* because life happened and managing your creative life on top of that was just too much for the moment. Allow yourself to collapse and spread out and take some notes so you don't run yourself into the ground next time.

If the story of the Wands was a movie, the Ten of Wands might make you think it had pacing issues. This ten comes on us so suddenly, but that's the way of fable. There were omens and portents the whole way through, and still this is where we ended up. Fire moves quickly, destructively, but there are always times we could have gotten it under control. There are no pacing issues here—only us, refusing to see what was really going on, refusing to take the right actions to prevent this. That's the lesson this fable leads us to—pay attention and treat the fire well.

We've looked at various facets of the Wands cards with every step, which included warnings to step back from our work or approach it differently. I remind you of that because with this Ten, maybe it's fine! Maybe this is simply the card that shows up when the work is completed. Maybe the one more straw to break the camel's back simply means we are done, and no more straws are necessary. You can see this a lot if your creative expression is writing: this is the place where you edit yourself to death and then wonder why the work is falling apart. The message itself is clear in this card though: take a break until you feel that inner flame flickering on its own again. Don't forget to pat yourself on the back for a creative job done on the way to your nap either!

Journey through the Wands Activities

1. **The Ten**—We aren't doing this for every suit, but I think the very real threat of burnout or being overtaken is ever present, so I want us to take a few moments to think about the last time we burnt out on creative projects. Look at (maybe even meditate on) your Ten of Wands card—or pull several from several decks to see where you see yourself. Journal or take some notes on why you ended up there, and what you could have done instead. Did you fail to put a structure in place that allowed you to follow through more easily? Was it too much too fast or a different pacing issue? Were you jumping into too many projects instead of following the flow on the biggest one that was coming through? There are no wrong

answers here but do take the time to figure out what you can do differently and how you can protect your precious spark moving forward.

2. **Tell a Different Story**—Now that you've seen both a mini narrative with our equation for creativity and a full interpretation of what a journey of the Wands might be or look like, remember that the whole point of this book is for you to learn how to use the tarot to exercise your own creativity. Take some time now to find a totally different story in the Wands, one that is all yours and tells of your own relationship to imagination, creation, or creative process. Use your tarot journal or scratch paper, and feel free to repeat this activity with the other suits as we go, tying their core messages to your artistic journey.

Getting to Know the Wands Suit

Card	Traditional Associations	Personal Associations
Ace of Wands	New ideas New opportunities Spark of passion or inspiration	
Two of Wands	Planning Putting passion into action Setting a path Decisions Discovery	
Three of Wands	Travel or wanderlust Expansion and growth Opportunities Progress	
Four of Wands	A big move or step forward Joy at home Cause for celebration and happiness	

Card	Traditional Associations	Personal Associations
Five of Wands	Conflict, including inner conflict Fighting or disagreements Stress or tension Nasty or petty competition	
Six of Wands	Victory and triumph Success Winning an inner battle Recognition Self-confidence	
Seven of Wands	Self-defense Standing up for what you believe in Challenge or competition Perseverance	
Eight of Wands	Busy, busy—everything taking off at once Swiftness and fast action Movement and change (though usually positive)	
Nine of Wands	Resilience and persistence Another fight, growing weary but you're almost at the finish line! Boundaries!	
Ten of Wands	Burnout or complete overwhelm Too many burdens Codependent or overly individualistic/solitary tendencies	

A Court of Wands

The Court Cards are the "other" four cards in your suit, usually labeled something like "Page/Knight/Queen/King." In the *Thoth Tarot* it's "Princess/Prince/Queen/Knight." In the tarot renaissance of the past several years, there are lots of beautiful decks renaming the court cards to get away from gender specificity. The *Slow Holler Tarot* uses Student, Traveler, Visionary, and Architect. *The Numinous Tarot* uses Dreamer, Explorer, Creator, and Mystic. In whatever deck you use, you'll recognize the Court Cards because they are labeled by name as opposed to the pips, which are labeled by numbers 1 through 10. There are a multitude of different ways to read the Court Cards and if you ask three tarot readers how to do so, you'll get nineteen different answers. One fun way to explore the Wands Court Cards is to think about all of the different ways we internalize that initial spark of inspiration.

The **Page of Wands**, for example, is really dancing with the original inspiration that we see in the Ace. This is internalization where we're riding out the ideas. Maybe we're starting several pencil sketches or drafts to see what sticks, for example. This is also the version of ourselves that sometimes hears the call to creative action and decides to go out and see what others are creating and doing first. This is surprisingly good research energy for a project but is best suited to taking in a lot of art and media for further inspiration.

The **Knight of Wands** on the other hand charges full steam ahead. This is the answer to the call that looks like staying up all night finishing a draft, or furiously getting all of our ducks in a row so we can create more fully the next day. This energy is absolutely not sustainable, but this Knight doesn't care. This Knight wants those ideas out of their mind and body right now and works seemingly tirelessly to make it so.

The **Queen of Wands** is more confident in both their ideas and their ability to see them to fruition. This Court Card is more likely to take their time and pace themself, while also making time for things that keep that spark going.

While follow-through is not the strong suit of any of the Wands Courts, this Queen is more likely to get restless or to try to follow a different muse on a hunch instead of burning out or becoming consumed.

The Queens in the tarot, like the Threes, correlate right back to The Empress. They often represent us internalizing the lessons from The Empress that we're trying to learn. So while the King might be all about sharing their creative ideas and productions with the world, the Queen has mastered the imagination and gotten a handle on how to really make something out of their spark. Because we are also focused on self-care in this book, we know that this Queen is not likely to hit that Ten of Wands burnout very often *because* they have internalized the lessons from The Empress on how to avoid that. They have put their raw energy and used it as motivation, while never sacrificing the carnal pleasure or indulgence that fires them right back up.

The **King of Wands** is gregarious and loves to share the whole creative process from spark to finish with others. That being said, this King is being fed a pretty consistent diet of ideas and inspiration from their inner flames. This King is an expert in how to follow your inspiration and put that inspiration into action. They see the full picture of the project and are able to direct others accordingly. When they do finish their work it is bold and cohesive, and the attention to detail will likely surprise people who expected more of a Knight energy from this card. This King can also help with group creative endeavors like theatre and dance.

Getting to Know the Wands Courts

In your pips, you laid out your cards and came up with some personal interpretations and associations for your cards. The Court Cards in the tarot have the potential to be even more personal and nuanced than the other tarot cards, so take some time now to lay yours out and really figure out how they're speaking to you based on what you've learned so far. Use the Wands Court Cards Activity that follows— it can help you if you get stuck.

Card	Traditional Associations	Personal Associations
Page of Wands	Free spiritedness Endless potential Happy playing with ideas and techniques before settling on one Able to go with the flow of the muse	
Knight of Wands	Fast action Works hard and fast but burns out or runs away easily Energy and passion Adventurous and impulsive	
Queen of Wands	Confidence in talents and visions Independence and determination Most evenly tempered of the Wands Courts Able to commute ideas and actions to near-completion	
King of Wands	Visions and visionaries Natural and generous leaders Gregariousness Honor, dignity, and surprisingly detailed	

Wands Court Cards Activities

1. While each Wands Court Card definitely has their own energy and ideas, we can see pieces of our process throughout them. Look at your Wands Courts in order, and then mix them up or put them in a circle to see how each energy feeds into the next one. What do you learn about your own habits when it comes to using inspiration through this examination?

2. The Court Cards often represent different sides of ourself that come out at various times. This is a great way to think of these cards as you're learning them, but in a creative context it can help to tie our understanding of the cards to what we've observed in characters from fiction or personalities from pop culture. In a lot of creative work, places are characters and take a shape all their own. Even events (especially inciting incidents in fiction) become characters all their own. Don't limit yourself to a character being human. A character is anything that has a distinct morality, mentality, and personality and that takes action to drive the story forward. If it helps you to limit this exercise to human or animal characters, that's okay, too.

    In either case, spend some time thinking about what characters from art, literature, or media match up to which of these Court Cards based on your understanding of them. Feel free to do this when we progress into the other suits as well. For extra credit, see if you see an archetype or other overarching creative element that that character connects to. This too will deepen your understanding of creating and of your tarot cards.

Wands Cards Spreads

Fanning Your Inner Flame Spread

This three-card spread helps you see, understand, and nurture your own creative fire.

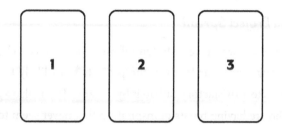

Card 1: Where in your body is your creative spark simmering, just aching to burst forth?

Card 2: How can you nurture this spark or flame?

Card 3: What comes from ongoing relationship with your inner flame or creative spark?

Into the Fire Spread

Once you've figured out what the burning urge to create is trying to tell you, this three-card spread helps you get started on the actual planning and action of creativity.

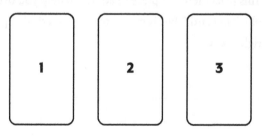

Card 1: What creative ideas are you trying to shape into something tangible?

Card 2: What media can you use to help you turn this raw creative notion into a creative outlet?

Card 3: Lay out between one and three cards to show you what steps you can take to go into the creative fire and make something out of it.

The Passion Project Spread

This is a spread for when we've bitten off more than we can chew in life; it helps us narrow down our focus to the projects most likely to sustain this energy and create a satisfactory catharsis by the end. This is also a good spread for those who are having bursts of inspiration that never seem to amount to anything.

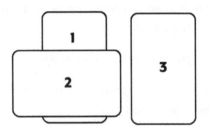

Card 1: Which passion projects are the right ones for you to focus on right now?

Card 2: What is blocking you from diving into those projects?

Card 3: This placement is a piece of advice to help you overcome the block in Card 2 but is meant to have practical applications right away.

Wands Self-Care Prompts

1. **Make plans to do something that gets your engines revving this week.** That might be a sexy outing with a partner, going to see a concert, or literally throwing a bonfire for your favorite people on a crisp autumn evening.

2. **If you're feeling tense and agitated, make what I call a "fuck this" list.** It's a list of everything that's pissing you off today. You're basically saying, "Fuck missing this bus, fuck being backed up at work, fuck the leak in the bathroom sink." When you're done, take a deep breath and move your pen back and forth scratching at all the writing on the paper. Then tear it up, crumble it up, throw it away, burn it (safely). Whatever you gotta do. You probably feel better now! Yay!

3. **Do something physical!** Run, use handbells, or dance loudly (I said what I said) in your living room until you break a sweat and feel like you've gotta stop. For those super pain-filled days, movement to me can mean pacing my apartment, stretching, or even just changing clothes. Just make sure you don't push yourself too hard or into injury (and obviously don't do anything you're not physically able to do safely).

Wands Creative Prompts

1. **Close your eyes and think about the word "fire."** Do you end up picturing a bonfire, a wildfire, a lit match, or something else entirely? Create a drawing or painting of what you see, even if that's not your usual medium, or bake something full of spice and heat. Then, write a poem about what you created even if *that's* not your usual medium.

2. **Create a cautionary tale about burnout.** Which tarot cards warn us that this Ten of Wands is coming? How can we avoid it *or* if we can't avoid it, how do we recover from it? Pour all of that into your creative piece.

3. **In a piece you're working on now, add something that you're passionate about exploring.** Maybe it won't make the final cut of the piece, maybe it will. In either case, add it now. This can be approaching a topic you've always wanted to explore in a subplot or playing with a favorite style for a visual piece. It's honestly just whatever sprang to mind when you heard "something you're passionate about exploring."

Wands Ritual: Intention Candles

This is perhaps the most obvious fire magic that we can draw on, but there is a reason to start our elemental rituals here. Fire magic is one of the most important aspects of both our practices, and so now is an ideal time to learn. In this ritual, you will dedicate a candle to your creative work. From here on out, as you work through the prompts and exercises in this book, you can burn your candle and feel the support of the suit of Wands as you do so.

As with everything in magic, start with setting an intention. Perhaps you have a specific creative project that you would like to dedicate this candle to, or maybe you want this candle to support you as you are trying to move past a creative block. This could also be a candle that you light to support your self-care practices. Take a few moments to think about what you might want this intention to be. If you are stumped and want something supportive, you can use this intention: "As I burn this candle, I recommit to creative self-expression."

Once you have the intention set, you can start to work with the candle.

Any candle will work for this ritual. If this is something that you will be working on for a longer period of time, I recommend choosing a larger pillar candle. If you want to see faster results, choose a smaller candle. When the candle burns all the way to the end, it will represent the magical completion of the spell.

Materials:

- A candle

- A lighter/matches

- A piece of paper

Step One: Choose an intention for this candle. If you are stumped, feel free to use this intention: "I express myself freely and creatively, connecting to my inner self. I affirm that I have something important to say."

Step Two: Hold the candle between your hands and connect with it. Repeat your intention over and over again into the candle.

Step Three: Write out the intention on a slip of paper, and then place it underneath the candle.

Step Four: Light the candle, and then go do your creative practice. If possible, light your candle every time you sit down to work on this practice.

9

SWORDS–CREATIVITY AND CLARITY THROUGH STRUGGLE

Swords are ideas, transformational pain, and finding a way to Truth.

Self-care is never more essential than when we are struggling. It's important to learn to practice self-care when we are feeling well, so that we can fall back on established self-care habits when we're going through a crisis. Tarot is one of the tools we can draw on for self-care. As we have already seen there are ample metaphors within the Major Arcana for difficulty and tragedy. "A Tower Moment" is a sort of pop-culture truism that tarot readers use to describe moments when it all falls apart.

The tools that we need to withstand our Tower Moments can also be found in the rest of the deck. The Empress, of course, is a card that helps us to connect with nourishment and care even in times of struggle. The Empress as an archetype knows that creativity is a powerful healer. They help us to cultivate our self-care in times of pleasure, as well as times of pain. The Star and Temperance both help us to slow down and rest and take a step back to gather our thoughts. Even in Tower times, The Star is available to us.

But how is this expressed in the Minor Arcana? Through the suit of Swords.

There are a lot of people who believe that creativity and the drive to make art stems from experiencing pain in our lives. The idea of the tortured artist looms large. We might think of people like Vincent Van Gogh and Frida Kahlo as examples of this kind of artist. Their work moves us, it helps us to process our own difficulties, and helps us to get through the hard times in our own lives.

While we don't believe that pain is a prerequisite of art, we *do* recognize that pain can be a catalyst—a motivation for intellectual and emotional exploration of the shadow side of the human experience.

You might find that having a creative outlet is essential for making it through troubled times. Sometimes you need the escape that the creative process provides—or you might need to watch your favorite comfort movies. Escapism does have its place, but that is not the domain of the suit of Swords. Still, different people process things differently; there are plenty of artists, writers, musicians, and other creatives who struggle to create when they are in pain. It's always important to make sure your needs are met. If your source of income is your creativity and if that is your primary struggle, you may have difficulty connecting to your creative spirit.

The suit of Swords is here to help us process our pain, and perhaps even release it into something greater. Swords include some of the most feared cards in the Minor Arcana, but it's important to remember that the tarot is here for all aspects of our lives. And so just as the Swords can offer up a mirror to your own struggles, they can also offer clarity to move through them and heal. Whether that happens during the Tower moments or after the dust has settled, the processing is an important aspect of it.

It's important to note that Swords are *forged*, meaning they are created through fire and metal coming together. The balance of a sword is essential to its use, and it is important to find the right sword for you. Each sword needs to be fitted to the person wielding it—based on their height, strength, and their need. The ideas that come through with the Swords are therefore also meant for you. They are the divine inspiration that can lead you forward.

In the Introduction, we talked about the equation for creativity: that you must subtract Judgment of Self from your mix of Imagination, Expression, and Reflection for the sum of creativity to be fully realized.

The Swords are a painful suit to work with sometimes, but the beauty of the Swords suit is greater than this pain. The Swords *do* help us to cut through the Judgment of Self and allow us to flourish more broadly, though they most closely connect to Reflection in this equation. While the Swords lay bare our demons, they also give us the tools necessary to slay them. That clarity is strong, and helps us communicate our desires, our needs, our ideas. It helps us to get that self-conscious part of ourselves out of the way.

Swords are related to the element of Air, helping us learn and communicate. Most art is our attempts to communicate something deep about ourselves or the way we see the world. It is through this act that we are able to process things around us, and we are even able to transmute our pain. *Communication and cognizance* of pain is truly what this suit is all about. Those ideas do not come without *Reflection*. Swords help us understand how to express those ideas—but the heart of them lies in Reflection.

Technology, which also correlates to Swords, simply represents the medium in which we create and communicate. So for a writer, this could obviously be using a computer to write. For a filmmaker it is the camera and other equipment that you use—and it is the script. For an artist, this can represent digital creative tools, but it can also represent that specific kind of paint that you prefer. Swords can indeed show up in a reading to show us a new mode of creation, a new innovation that we want to use as we are creating.

Technology is similar to the word technicality, which is also an application of the Swords cards. Here we are applying technical skill to our creative spark. This is the suit of learning the guitar, not just writing music or lyrics. In theatre, this is the structure that plays are written in and based on and the acting styles that are used. Both technology and technicality help us analyze our creative work and make decisions about what we really want to do. The suit of Swords can bring us a certain level of clarity around why we are creating, what we want to create, and also *how* we want to create.

Unlike Cups, which is exalted creative expression, Swords deal with the nitty-gritty of it—the actual words we use, the technical skill applied to our creative skill set, and the technology we use to broadcast it. Finely tuned skills and intellect are prized here, and this ties back to the mind's work of reflection in our equation. Reflection in the Swords is processing, synthesizing, and simply taking the time to be with your thoughts.

Whether this is your first time meeting the Swords, or your five-hundredth, there is new meaning in each card as you approach them again.

. . . .

Styles of witchcraft to play with: Sigils, smoke scrying, automatic writing, mantras and incantations, magical songs, storm spells. Using incense and burning herbs for cleansing.

. . . .

. . . .

Styles of creativity to play with: Automatic writing, journaling, poetry, story craft, any kind of writing—swords are extremely word-related. Blending scents, like with perfumery or incense. Reading something in the genre you want to write in. Or, conversely, reading something in a genre you *don't* write in. Reading about your favorite creators.

. . . .

. . . .

Other tarot cards that notably feature Air or Swords: Justice, Judgment, the Knights, The Magician

. . . .

The Journey through the Swords

The story of the Swords is a story of moving through pain, processing that trauma, and innovation. Depending on whether you're looking at this more as a suit of innovation and technology or as mental illness and traumatic history, and depending on the question you ask the cards, this suit tells multiple stories. Those stories have a tendency to get mixed together. Nothing is ever created in a vacuum; everything is a web that weaves into itself over and over again.

The other thing to keep in mind is that stories can be nonlinear. So even though we are writing about the cards in numerical order to make them accessible for learners, it doesn't necessarily mean that you have made it through the energy of the card before and aren't looking forward to the energy of the card after. For example, if you pull the Four of Swords, it doesn't necessarily mean that you are healing from a Three of Swords moment. So many of the cards in this particular story are signs that you might be headed for disaster if you don't heed their warnings, rather than a fatalist prescription. We don't need to end up at the Ten of Swords, with release and failure and pain as the final chapter of this story. At the same time, so often these cards—particularly the really difficult ones like that Three or Ten of Swords—help us process the very real shit we go through.

So, with that, here is a linear telling of the story of the Swords. It is a story full of warning, omens, and ultimately—release.

We start with the **Ace of Swords**. This card can feel a bit jarring when we look at the story as a whole, but it's important to remember that the Aces contain all of the *potential* of the suit ahead. The Ace of Swords is the flash of inspiration, the challenge, the cutaway, the release, and the clarification of the suit all rolled into one. This is a surefire sign that inspiration is on its way like a strike of lighting. Many times, when I (Siri) pull the Ace of Swords I feel excited and giddy to see what comes next. But that is only one side of the blade.

This Ace also knows pain from a deep, deep level. When you see this card and feel that sinking feeling, it is your intuition telling you that there is a difficult time ahead. As much as the Ace holds all of the inspiration of the suit of Swords, it also holds the pain of this suit. One side of this sword is that flash of inspiration, and the other side is all of that doubt, judgment, and fear. It may be a distant memory of pain once felt, or perhaps that pain sears all around you. The Ace of Swords can also represent a clean break. It cuts through the bullshit to get to something closer to your ideal.

Where we really begin to step forward is with the **Two of Swords.** In the classic Rider-Waite-Smith deck, we see a figure blindfolded and holding two swords crossed over their heart. In the background is a lake with rock outcroppings and a waxing crescent moon above. In terms of our creative life, the Two of Swords represents an invitation into our unconscious, where we aren't able to see what's ahead. Because it is a Two, this card is connected with The High Priestess—one who stands firm in their intuition. The Two of Swords takes time to truly contemplate all of the options. This can also represent setting boundaries. One of my favorite ways of looking at this card is verbally setting boundaries with people so that we can have the space we need to think our way through the problems at hand. It's turning inward when we need to and carving out that space for ourselves. Other keywords for this card include: consideration, stagnancy, and a truce.

The **Three of Swords** is one of the most traditional heartbreak cards. It most often shows a floating heart, with three swords piercing it and rain clouds all around. This comes when we realize that something we really care about just isn't working. This is that moment in a creative project where you realize it's not only not working, but also unsalvageable. If your creative projects are collaborative in nature, like performance art, this might indicate a breakup of the collaborating partners. The Three of Swords can also represent a betrayal, like being stabbed in the back on a project. It is also important to note that this is just the three—it isn't the final release of the Ten of Swords yet. It is a setback or a breakup that *feels* more intense than it actually is in a lot of cases. When this comes up in a reading, be very aware of any relationship dynamics or people that are in a position of betraying your trust.

This Three relates back to The Empress, but it shows some of the pain that comes with being The Empress. It's important to remember that The Empress is powerful, is large and in charge, and knows what they deserve. That does not mean this always comes easy. It does not mean that the metaphorical gardens so often shown with The Empress do not put out bad crops or rotten fruit sometimes. The lesson here is not just that life is hard regardless of our work. When we're looking at interpersonal relationships, the combination of the Three of Swords with The Empress is the difficult lesson that sometimes living your truth means breaking up with that significant other who isn't right, no matter how cute they are (for example). In order to fully embody The Empress, we have to be willing to call things when they are done, to move on after a trying time, and to let things be bad sometimes without fighting it. It's only in that work that we make room for all of the beautiful creations we are yet to put out.

The **Four of Swords** represents rest. It typically shows someone lying down, but one sword is close and at the ready. Coming straight after heartbreak, this feels like the rest and recuperation necessary to continue on in your creative pursuit. Depending on the art on your particular card, this could also be interpreted as a creative block. In this case, you are incorporating harsh truths that were perhaps revealed in the breakup that was the Three of Swords. This card almost always indicates a need to slow down and really take your time before moving forward. Make sure you're ready before taking action. Other keywords for this card: peace, healing, planning.

The **Five of Swords** can be read in a lot of different ways, but given our focus, I think of this card as picking up the pieces after writer's block or a creative partnership breakup. So if you have suffered a loss at this point, it's a retreat and an attempt to gather yourself again. This could also be a failure in a business venture. Do you see yourself in the figure picking up the swords or in the figures retreating? This can tell you so much about a particular situation. This is another card that can represent betrayal and perhaps even self-sabotage. There is a certain aspect of this card related to jealousy—particularly envy of the progress that others are making or the assets they have. When I think about that in terms of the creative process, I think of this as being unable to see the value in your own work, and instead comparing yourself to other people too much. When you're in the middle of a creative process, there's a certain amount of keeping your eyes on your own project that is essential to enjoying the process.

The **Six of Swords** is sometimes seen as another despair card in the tarot. Sixes often represent a reprieve between major challenges, so this is the time right after a traumatic event when the tears flow and all of those emotions come rushing back. If you haven't been able to actually emotionally process something intense, those emotions come through when you are finally able to rest. Yet this card shows someone helping you. Often pictured are one to two figures sitting down in a boat. They are shrouded, downtrodden, and fully in their grief process. The person rowing the boat is there to help guide them. This could mean reaching out to a friend when you are so thoroughly in the creative process that you can't see the good things about your work, and it could also be transporting yourself into a different place with your work. Sometimes the only way out is through, and you just need to finish that draft or concept sketch.

Another reading of this card emphasizes that while despair is in the past, we are moving away from it now into unknown territory. This is scary and hard, and often leads us to want to react defensively or even go on the offense like the upcoming Seven. Where we're moving to is definitively better than where we've been, and the card encourages us to embrace whatever is coming. In terms of self-care, this means releasing the pain from the past (potentially using therapy and medicine if needed, also indicated in the Swords) and trying to accept the current journey for what it is.

The **Seven of Swords** is a rush, running away from the past and toward an uncertain future. It can often manifest as running away and avoiding previous bad decisions, attempting to look the other way when you need to take responsibility. This is another one of those warning cards. The warning here is really to slow down and think about what you're doing. When I think about the Seven of Swords in my own creative process, I think about it as refusing to look back over my work. "I don't need to edit this—I'm done," when in fact there are massive plot holes and whole sentences left unfinished. This could also be refusing to take constructive criticism seriously even when you know that it would dramatically improve the quality of your work. Another way this card could manifest in your creative life is through taking on too many projects at once and not being able to see them through without dropping the quality of your work. Because this is the suit of Swords, it can represent an overabundance of ideas and being unclear which ideas to say "yes" to.

The **Eight of Swords** is a card that can be haunting. This card traditionally shows someone bound, blindfolded, and amongst eight swords sticking out of the ground. But one important thing to note about this illustration in many decks is that it doesn't show any swords directly in front of the figure. There's a certain amount of being blocked when this card comes up *and* a certain amount of need to trust in your intuition. Even if you can't see the path forward, there is one. There is another sort of almost sacrifice related to this card: sometimes you have to fall on your sword to move forward. This is a theme that comes back in the Ten of Swords. This is not a comfortable place to find yourself, and it can indeed mean that there are very real blocks. It also might mean sacrificing something that you really care about in order to progress. I've found that when this card is present, there's a lot of worry. This is a card of obsession, of trying to open the puzzle box without having the key. When you can't see the answer clearly, you might have a tendency to obsess over what it could possibly be. The remedy for this is finding some space.

The **Nine of Swords** is a nightmare card. This is feeling completely immobilized with fear. This is a moment when trauma or pain is driving your responses, when the present situation blends with a past horrific situation. This is not necessarily a card of new trauma or pain but of being haunted in its aftermath. You may be blaming yourself for what happened, even though it is very far beyond your control. In creative terms, this is what we face when we aren't able to work through our traumas or other painful events from our past. They continue to plague us. The story of the swords isn't linear, and it's very likely that in transmuting your pain into your creative life you will be experiencing that pain anew. A remedy for this is remembering that the swords are on the wall—that when it's too much, you can put them back there. This is also a card of confrontation—you can't avoid the trauma in your life, past mistakes, the wrong that you have perpetrated, or that others have done to you.

Finally, the **Ten of Swords** represents the ultimate release of the Swords suit. The card shows a figure lying face down in the mud with ten swords in their back. In the background is either a sunrise or a sunset, depending on your perspective. The card often represents death to rebirth. If the project that you've been creating has centered around themes of pain and trauma, this is that final push to process your subject matter and release it into the world. This can have you feeling extra vulnerable.

So often this kind of creativity comes from such a personal place that it can feel incredibly challenging to have new eyes on it. Know that you have done all you can at this time and do your best to release your fears of being seen. This could also represent a tragic end to a cycle. As much as this card is about death and rebirth, the emphasis is on death. Some of our stories are tragedies, and it's important to hold space for that ending that hurts. The Ten of Swords can also represent a metaphorical postpartum depression—the intense sadness that comes when you've finished something and put it out in the world and are at loose ends. This is a side of creating that we don't often talk about, but there is an aimless feeling at the end of a major project. Give yourself space to grieve.

Getting to Know the Swords Suit

Go through your own Swords suit, lay them all out, and figure out what your personal associations are with these cards. Also take note of any primary symbols that draw your focus. Check back into the Traditional Associations as a point of reference but do your own research and write down keywords that are specific to your deck and your own interpretations.

Card	Traditional Associations	Personal Associations
Ace of Swords	Associated with The Fool A flash of insight, new idea, intellectual undertaking The potential to become a thought leader in your field The cycle of a new revelation in mental health	

Card	Traditional Associations	Personal Associations
Two of Swords	A choice—especially between two bad situations Setting boundaries Turning inwards—especially as a defense Duality Disconnect between situation and logic	
Three of Swords	Deep sadness plus loss Expansion of the consequences of bad choices Turning to anger as an expression of sadness Heartache Drama	
Four of Swords	Rest and recovery Recuperation for a brief time Returning to logic Getting stable once more	
Five of Swords	Unfair advantage Being resentful of what others have A loss in a situation An empty victory Picking up the pieces even when you don't want to	
Six of Swords	Grief journey Relying on others to help us through grief Ability to move on after struggle Travel Finding peace in a difficult situation	

Card	Traditional Associations	Personal Associations
Seven of Swords	Betrayal and deception Running away from past bad decisions Unwilling to face the truth Not looking where you're going Chaotic thinking, inability to focus	
Eight of Swords	Mentally bound or imprisoned Paralyzed—unable to take a step forward Turning away from support system Unable to see situation clearly Unable or unwilling to use available tools to help you	
Nine of Swords	Being haunted by a sense of loss Blaming the self for what has happened, even if it was beyond your control Anxiety Lack of control over difficult situations	
Ten of Swords	Defeat, which releases you into the next cycle Retaliation Hope: you have an answer, and can put this matter behind you Death to rebirth Release	

A Court of Swords

The Court Cards of this suit are really here to help us navigate the issues the Swords suit brings up. They are aspects of self and both creative and divine archetypes that we can draw on. Sometimes they represent personal or spirit allies, and sometimes they represent IRL allies.

The **Page of Swords** is perhaps the most lighthearted of the Swords court. They are extremely curious, intellectually inquisitive, always asking the question "why?" This card can feel really separate from the energy of the Swords court overall. However we can see this card as a genuine exploration of the limits of human understanding. That is no small task.

The Page of Swords can also be laughing to get through traumatic situations and maintain the heart to keep going. They have a curiosity to see what's on the other side of this challenge. It is this spirit that also helps us apply our own difficult experiences to the stories we tell. "What if this happened, but differently?" The Page of Swords is an ally that reminds you to look at different sides of the story, and to expand your understanding of the events that have led you to create. This Page is very good for lightening the mood when you are feeling blocked or burdened.

The **Knight of Swords** is the fastest moving of the knights. This Knight is often shown charging forward, the landscape in the card whipping past them. We like to think of the Knight of Swords as representing the Air card in the Air-elemented court. So of course they're fast-moving. They're quick-witted and get their words out, often without considering the consequences. When thinking of trauma-informed Court Cards, the Knight of Swords is the one who leads with their experiences without thinking of whether the person they're speaking with can hold that kind of space. In contrast, in terms of the creative process, the Knight of Swords is a fantastic ally in finishing. Get that messy first draft done, make a bunch of concept sketches, spend the first 10 minutes in the dance studio playing around. Get your juices flowing. Your brain will catch up later.

The **Queen of Swords** is an old friend, the queen of boundaries. This card is the tough-love face of The Empress, but we do not want to lose sight of the love they offer. In the Rider-Waite-Smith deck, they hold their sword straight, pointed at the sky. This is reminiscent of the Justice card in the Major Arcana, which also tells us that this Queen is concerned with ultimate Truth. This can be harsh—sometimes we are the ones who are not being true to ourselves or who need an awakening. The Queen of Swords is also a really good ally for helping you to express the boundaries that you need to set. So often, creative burnout comes from not taking time away from your creativity, or not allowing yourself the space for creativity. The Queen of Swords can help you set boundaries that will allow you the time necessary for your creations.

The **King of Swords** is a stoic friend and ally. They are pictured facing the reader in the Rider-Waite-Smith deck so they can be an outward face, whereas the Queen is more about internal processes. In terms of artistic process and working through pain in your art, the King of Swords helps you connect with your audience without getting hurt when they talk back. The King of Swords is able to handle and deal with criticism fairly. This is a major part of any creative project that goes public, and so it is important to work with this energy. The King can help you get your work in front of the people that need to see it and handle the vulnerability of putting yourself out there.

Getting to Know the Swords Court

Like the exercise above with the pips, take out your court cards. Look at them, turn them over, and get to know their personality. This can look like literally having a conversation with the court cards, looking at the other symbols on the cards to get a sense of their personalities, and perhaps even free journaling about your relationship to the court cards.

Card	Traditional Associations	Personal Associations
Page of Swords	Ambitions Swift judgment Communication Intellectual curiosity	
Knight of Swords	Warrior Charging forward Intellectual aggression Speaking before thinking	
Queen of Swords	Astute Boundary enforcer High-achieving Independent	
King of Swords	A leader in the intellectual field Analytical Stern	

Swords Court Cards Activities

This will heavily rely on journaling and timing as a way of connecting with the sometimes-severe Swords Court. Make sure that you have a pen, paper, and a way of keeping time. Isolate the Swords Court from the rest of your deck. Lay them out in order.

Pick up the Page of Swords. Set a timer for 1 minute, and spend that minute staring at the card, immersed in it. When the minute is over, pick up your pen and paper and set a timer for between 1 and 5 minutes. Freewrite across the page, never allowing pen to leave paper. If that means you write scribbles, then you write scribbles. Write out any impressions after engaging with the Page, any questions you might want to ask them, and any notes on their personality after sitting with them.

Do this for the rest of the Swords court.

Look over what you've written for each of the Swords and how you might work best with them. Think of these as different personalities that you could be working with. What have you learned about the court cards in your specific deck? How do you think you can communicate with them moving forward?

Swords Spreads

Mental Clarity Spread

If you're anything like us, you may have a lot of ideas at once. Those Aces of Wands and Swords might be a little too generous with sharing ideas with you. This spread can help you figure out what ideas to follow right now.

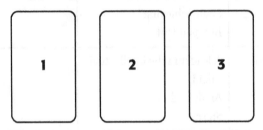

Card 1: What is your most important idea right now?

Card 2: What do you need to learn to move forward?

Card 3: What is your next best step?

Sharp Realization Spread

This spread will help you cut through the brain fog and get to that essential truth of a situation. This can help even outside of your creative life—use this spread when you're really confused about what the best process for moving forward is. This spread (shown on page 119) also helps you to identify why it's difficult for you to think through this stuff, which is extremely helpful.

Card 1: What is the underlying truth of this situation?

Card 2: What is blocking me from seeing the truth?

Card 3: What can I do about it?

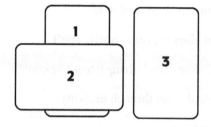

A Spread for Managing Pain in Creative Process

Whether you're dealing with writer's/artist's block, doubting yourself as a creator, or figuring out new ways of using past pain in your work, this spread can help smooth some of the edges for you.

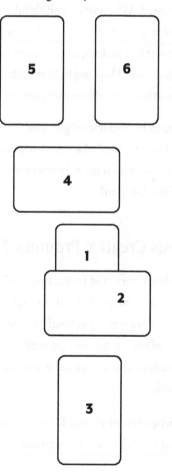

Card 1: Your current emotional state

Card 2: What is blocking your creative spirit

Card 3: The Shadow—underlying issues to examine

Card 4: The Sword—cut through to clarity

Card 5: Next best step

Card 6: How to heal and move forward long-term

Swords Self-Care Prompts

1. **A journaling prompt:** When you think about art through pain, what art or media works stand out to you? How do you feel about those works? Break down some of the technique that went into that work and apply it to a piece of your own. How might that system provide depth to your work and an opportunity to release that pain for yourself?

2. **Where do you need boundaries right now?** This might be in protecting one area of your life, or it might be self-disciplinary. How do the Swords teach you to set and maintain those boundaries? What do they show you about the payoff for doing so?

Swords Creative Prompts: Memoir

As we've seen, Swords are very tied to the mind, which is where memory is stored. This makes Swords the perfect suit to explore memoir and personal storytelling. Even if you are not a personal storyteller, come up with some quick answers to the following memoir prompts to drive home the Swords lessons from The Empress. You can either use just your Swords for these or work with a whole deck.

1. **Embrace an Embodiment prompt.** Pull a tarot card and find a way to (comfortably and safely) take on the position and posture of the card's

primary figure. Stay in the position you're in for a bit. How does it feel in your body? What does it look or feel like you're doing or about to do? Really sit in this position. Then, write about a time you were in this position or doing an action implied by the position. Ask yourself, "Why was I doing this, and why does it live in my memory?" and "What lesson did I learn from this story?" Those last two questions really sum up what memoir is in the smallest of nutshells so let that lead you to *how* you write or tell this memory. We talk more about embodiment in Appendix 2 on Creative Approaches to the Tarot (see page 179).

2. **Try a Tarot Memoir prompt.** For this prompt, we're looking for something that is both story and memory. The best memoir pieces reflect on not only what we did but why we did it and what we learned. With that fresh in your mind, pull a tarot card. Use your understanding of the card to write or tell a memory where you learned the message of the card the hard way, and how that changed and shaped who you are now.

Swords Ritual: Create a Sigil

Sigils are some of the most direct ways that we can access Air energy in our magic. Just as the suit of Swords so often represents the written word and communication, sigil craft takes our intentions and transforms them into a symbol. Quite literally!

What is a sigil?

A sigil is a symbol that you create that represents the intention behind your magic. You charge your sigil so it has the power of your magic, and then you can carry it with you, carve it on a candle, or burn it.

Here's how to craft one:

Step One: Decide on an intention. If you are having trouble with this, you can use this intention: "I am able to understand and communicate my needs."

Step Two: Write out your intention in the present tense, then cross out all double letters.

"I am ble to undrs c y"

Step Three: Optional: Cross out all vowels.

"m bl t ndrs c"

Step Four: Create a symbol that is a combination of all of these letters together.

Step Five: Charge the sigil. This could look like pushing energy into the symbol, or leaving it out under a full moon, or anointing it with an oil that matches your intention.

Step Six: You can carry this sigil around with you. Write it on your body in pen, write it down in a notebook, write it on a slip of paper and put it in your phone case. When you feel that the sigil's intention has been accomplished, burn the sigil.

10

CUPS–THE CRUX OF SELF-EXPRESSION

The themes inherent to Cups are Beauty and Art,
Emotions and Expression, and Relationships.

 hen we think about creativity as seen in the tarot, the Cups suit has a well-deserved reputation for its reminders of beauty, art itself, and the importance of self-expression. For those of us whose disciplines are collaborative, Cups as the suit of relationships also makes it an easy translator for dealing with problem collaborators or feeling out how we'll work best with a group of people. The tarot itself tells a seventy-eight–card story, and when it comes to creativity, if Wands are that creative energy, raw and ready to burst, then Cups are about the self-expression and artwork that come from that.

Cups correlate to water, and in water we find all of these ideas *and* we find love of creating. We find a "heart's desire" type longing that feeds so much of our artistic expression. We find integrated intuition spurring on our ideas. Of course, the heart's desire and integrated intuition tag right back into the primary messages of Cups, which are tied up in emotional processes and expression of self. One of the things we love most about tarot is the way the ideas feed each other, and that is seen clearly in the Cups cards. Cups are about the artwork we take in and how it helps soothe our souls. In turn, this influences our creative output. It also affects our decision whether to show our own finished work to the world or not. Often we make that decision depending on what our heart was trying to express in the creative process. All of this is seen in these cards, and we'll explore that when we break down the journey of the Cups.

The Cups urge us to seek and celebrate beauty wherever we can find it. Art doesn't have to be beautiful. Self-expression *is* beautiful on its own. Art *is* beautiful on its own. Our creative process *is* beautiful on its own. The way art and creativity can help us express ourselves *is* beautiful. Art and creativity allow us a catharsis based on someone else's expression and that, too, *is* beautiful. Collaborative art is beautiful. So is solitary art. As you move through this book, don't get caught up by the word "beauty"—but the Cups want you to think about it.

Beauty does not need to have one concrete meaning, and the Cups urge us to explore what we mean when we say beauty. As we queer beauty or approach it from an anti-capitalist point of view, for example, what do we see? What do we find beautiful in decay, destruction, deconstruction? What creative ideas of your own do you connect beauty to or think others will find beauty in? The goal of the Cups cards is not to enforce a patriarchal standard of beauty on your work. It is to help you figure out what beauty means to you and to help you find the beauty in your process and output. The Cups want you to build creative projects in your own image, and they want you to recognize that as an act of power and beauty all its own.

Take a few moments to journal on what art you find beautiful, ironically or literally.

Of course, a lot of tarot learners and writers focus heavily on Cups as a suit that prioritizes relationships with others and love of all types. I actually think this is another reason we so heavily place the Cups alongside creative work. For most of us, we think of the great romances in movies before we think of another idea or theme that the movie focused on. We think of love songs first when we're thinking of music. This is a generalization, of course, and a lot of people are love- or romance-averse, but there is a beauty connected to love that shines through these cards and creative work that focuses on that theme.

Be challenged to focus more on relationships *of all types* as we work through the Cups and come to think of them as not as an expression of cis-heteronormative romantic love but as a suit that can guide us to finding the best collaborators for our creative life. The Cups can help us negotiate who does what creatively, and Cups can help us figure out who we'd make beautiful creations with. We see this in the Ace, where there's a potential outpouring of love and mutual support on a project, all the way through to the Ten, where we are satisfied and transformed by a project taken on with other people.

Styles of witchcraft to play with: Tinctures, oil mixes, potions, baths/showers/dips in the lake, coffee spells, and tea as a spell. You can get creative mixing spells with seltzer or other liquids, too, and magical mixology for those who drink alcohol. Florida water and floor washes in general fit here. Moon magic is a really common form of watery magic as the Moon dictates the tides.

Styles of creativity to play with: Mixing drinks (including teas, coffee creations, and mocktails), writing songs or poetry, music in general, dramedy in TV/film/theatre, journaling, anything that makes you cry happy or sad tears, paint (especially watercolor).

Other tarot cards that notably feature Cups or Water: Temperance, The High Priestess, The Star, The Moon, Six of Swords

The Journey through the Cups

There is a plethora of stories to choose from when we're going through the Cups' pips. We could tell the story of creative work from idea through completion, or the journey of emotional healing. We could go through a story about creating with our favorite collaborators. We encourage you to explore these stories and some that you come up with in your cards. This is such a beautiful way to learn and grow more deeply in your tarot know-how, and it will only benefit you.

For the purposes of this book, our Cups story is focused on the journey of learning to get comfortable expressing ourselves, and from that, learning it's okay to create for the sake of creating or for our own personal catharsis. So many of the most brilliant think-outside-the-boxers, be they artists, writers, and creators struggle with making things, and even more struggle with confidence in their creations. The synthesis of the suit of Cups, especially with The Empress's influence, is meant to lead us to more assertively make, do, create, and express. This means learning that if it comes from within us, it is beautiful. That is healing, and it exists in relationship with others, and it certainly takes us on the journey of the Cups.

Even though we're telling the story of the Cups in numerical order, Cups, more so than any other suit, really embrace fluid story structure. If you could even name the story structure of the Cups, it would be closer to surrealism than anything else.

Surrealism is thought of as an artistic movement with dreamlike (or nightmare-esque, depending on your viewpoint) images and literature. That was only a piece of what was actually a larger cultural movement that was striving to make sense of being a human after World War I. Surrealist artists *were* inspired by Dadaism (an "anything goes" avant-garde art movement from the 1910s), but they were also inspired by the esoteric and a potential connection between different worlds and states of reality. Surrealism actively wanted to activate the unconscious mind through imagery. Cups are meant to do a lot of the same things. Cups often represent higher self-intuition, which also relies on the subconscious and connection between different planes of existence. Our feelings are much more sacred than we give them credit for, and though this suit is also relegated to be "just" about our feelings, when it comes to self-expression and even basic self-care those feelings *are* the missing link. This is not simple emotions—it is the deep, profound way we feel and how that impacts everything from our spirituality to which jobs we choose (if we're privileged enough to be able to choose our jobs).

Examples of this nonlinear, fluid storytelling include the Six, which jerks us back in memory, and the Three, which can often feel like more of a subplot than a consequential next step. The Seven can easily be seen as a dream sequence; it's one of the cards that befuddle new readers the most. It also leans into an almost absurdist creative framework because of all the bizarre, seemingly unconnected items stuck in each cup in most decks. While often these things are deeply connected or represent a different part of your psyche, many times they are not.

Explore the journey we've written out here, and then explore mixing the cards up a little to see how they reveal themselves anew.

We start of course, with the **Ace of Cups**. The Aces in the tarot unlock something new for us. They are opportunities. They are chances to go on an adventure in line with the values of the suit. They are a way to look at things differently, through the eyes of the suit. In the case of the Ace of Cups, an ideal or desire is expressing itself for the first time or in a totally new way.

The Cups are often seen as a suit highlighting the emotional journeys we go on. The Ace can then be interpreted as an outpouring of emotion that we need to tend to. Making space for and taking care of our emotional selves is one of the most fundamentally important aspects of self-care, and the Ace offers us a chance to do just that. The Ace brings forth new emotions and desires to be expressed. It also brings forth the pitfalls of that—vulnerability. Giving in to our most difficult desires. Visibility of our feelings, and the backlash that may create. Yet Cups is a suit that ends with true happiness. The process might sting. You might lose something or someone. It will certainly be challenging to dive into this suit and gain confidence for self-expression. It will also be so worth it in that, by the end, it will be unbelievable that you almost skipped out on this journey out of fear.

We immediately see some "beginner's luck" in the **Two of Cups**. The Two indicates a good balance of emotions. It's often thought of as a relationship that is well-aspected, like you've met your match. In other words, you've used that opportunity of the Ace to strike a balance. Everything is in its place, emotionally speaking, and beautiful things are happening all around you as a result. Or maybe you're just noticing the beauty and the balance more. As a story of building toward greater self-expression, this is a really good place to push a little bit past your comfort level. For the relationships that are safe and balanced in your life, this is the time to share your wildest dreams or most uncomfortable feelings. When you get that affirmation, you'll feel stronger to continue the journey. As creative people, this also means approaching collaborators you think you'd work well with or sharing your brilliant albeit emotional ideas with someone you trust. They're likely able to offer feedback that not only feels good, but also keeps things balanced for now.

The **Three of Cups** is a stepping-stone in our journey to confidence in self-expression. This is a happy card of communing with others, of finding like-minded people. For readings on collaborative efforts, this is a good omen. As we take bold but cautious steps toward true freedom of expression, this is one of our favorite energies. This card is staying up all night brainstorming with friends and laughing. This is creating something brilliant after too many drinks or cups of coffee with a friend. This is finding your people, your group of dreamers and artists that makes you see that anything is possible, and it is reveling in that feeling. It is then allowing that to push you forward.

When we think about the Threes as expressions of The Empress, we see how important the relationships we have are; they reflect what we deserve back to us. We see that sacred time to dance and drink the water from these beautiful goblets feeds our creative soul. Allowing other people to take care of you is an absolutely necessary aspect of self-care. Accepting help, pleasure, and joy from others is one of the greatest gifts life can offer us. However, this acceptance is its own journey—and one The Empress is happy to lead us on.

Of course, as the Two taught us, life and emotions really are about balance. The **Four of Cups** and then the Five are kind of a crash from the elevated happy emotions the One, Two, and Three cards build on. The Four is a softer crash, but it is a feeling that kind of leaves us feeling like "well, now what?" We feel like we've said what needs to be said, like all the good ideas are taken or have run their course. There's a disconnect between our desire and our ability to express ourselves here, and there's a disconnect between a project we thought would make us happy and being able to feel that joy internally. In most Four of Cups images, there's a hand holding out a new goblet for you to grab. This is a chance to refresh with the cool beverage in question, and from that refreshed state reevaluate the plan.

If we choose not to reevaluate or are unable to see this downswing in mood as an opportunity, it leads us to the shadow aspects of the **Five of Cups**. This is heartache, loss. There's a message of release that is trying to come through in this card. In our case, it might mean letting go of projects that aren't working. It might mean living in the state of vulnerability that comes after we put ourselves out there. Sometimes we see bad emotions as an aspect of our identity when in fact, it is possible to release them. If you *do* choose to take the opportunity in the Four of Cups, you find a true release and catharsis in the Five of Cups. Sometimes our words or ideas get away from us in the best way possible, and in this case, taking a step back to reconsider what you want to say and how you want to say it allows a blissful, if bittersweet, release. You've looked at what you've created and how you've expressed yourself. You get it now.

We often teach the Sixes as how we pick ourselves up from the mess of the Fives, and in some ways that holds true here. The **Six of Cups** can be all about nostalgia, for better or worse. This Six is memory, tingling at the back of our neck, perhaps moving through our subconscious the way surrealist concepts do and flowing out onto the page, stage, or stove top. When we think about creating through the collective subconscious or ancestral memory, this is the Six of Cups.

This Six is a childlike energy, and one thing I think about a lot from a lens of creativity or self-expression is how taking in art or media we loved when we were younger can feed us in new ways as we age. We see things in the work we've never seen before, and we realize we maybe have something to say about that. It could also inspire ideas for expression and creation that we had the first time we embraced this art or media, bringing a new sight and maturity to a once-forgotten idea.

Because the Cups represent beauty—sometimes in service of overcoming pain—the Six of Cups is a good reminder to embrace what is still good and beautiful. When the going gets tough . . . sometimes the tough need to head to a museum, to nature, or to another place that speaks to them and fills them to the brim with satisfaction. The Six of Cups speaks to this as a way not only to heal from the pain or release of the Five, but also to find new ways of expression, forgotten ways of being, and a renewed vision for creation.

But healing from creative burnout or difficulty is not a linear process, which is why we hit the **Seven of Cups** next. This is another card that has really beautiful sides and difficult sides. This can definitely be a card of overwhelm. When we're working toward a greater sense of confidence in self-expression, this card expresses the burden of having too many things to say and no idea how to say them. Other common interpretations of this card show daydreaming and "head in the clouds" mentality. In our hyper-capitalist society, that is often seen as A Bad Thing. As creative people we know better. Daydreams inspire us, and no great artist has their feet 100 percent on the ground, and you will never convince us otherwise. You have to dream big and aim high. Even if you are not a career creative, even if you have no desire to monetize your great letter-writing or collage-creating skills, you deserve to indulge that daydreamy energy. It is your birthright to enjoy time fantasizing and dreaming about what you might create one day. It is only from this place that you'll be able to move on into the eight.

The **Eight of Cups** very often shows someone leaving eight cups, some of them shattered, as they head toward unknown territory. The metaphor is obvious: a bittersweet ending. For a lot of tarot clients, they see the amicable end of a relationship with a future unknown. This can and does include work relationships, too. Esoterically this is often the card that shows up when we have healed some inner wounds and can move forward into unknown spiritual territory. It takes so much of our lives to learn the lessons of cards One through Seven that we have literally never thought about what comes next. In the Eight, we are ready to not only embrace but also go in search of whatever is next. As a story of gaining confidence for self-expression, this hits deeply for a lot of us. We use the words we learn online, or from art teachers or therapists or other creatives in the earlier cards. Now after giving in to our heart's daydreams and meanderings we have new and authentic things to say that are just us. Furthermore, we are ready to take those things into the next chapter of our lives.

The **Nine of Cups** often gets overlooked as just a card about happiness and wishes coming true. It is often referred to as the "wish" card. When a client gets this card, readers often say that what the client wants the cards to say is showing up for them. The cards just may not be giving many details to the reader. This interpretation *is* true! But there's more! Wishes rarely come true for no reason. You've most likely suffered in your life; most of us have. In this story, you've suffered in the Five of Cups, maybe even in the Four through Seven of Cups. The Eight is not easy for you, and there are a lot of tears and nights of panic leading up to the break and new horizons. This Nine is not acquired simply. You earn it by learning to find your voice and strength in the face of oppression, trauma, or pain. It is a gift, but more than that it is a relief. It is when we know we will be okay. Expressing all of the beautiful thoughts and emotions you have swirling around inside of you is no easy feat. It's not easy to gain the confidence to express them, but when you do, you hit this Nine.

As we journey toward joy and happiness in self-expression, spend some time in this Nine. It feels like second nature to express yourself now, second nature to pour yourself into your creations. Yet it didn't always. You worked hard to get here. To that end, we'd say this is a card of expression for the sake of expression, art for the sake of art, doing wacky new things solely to try wacky new things.

As you indulge in that Nine, you'll notice something moving and shifting in you as we move toward the Ten. The **Ten of Cups** is often seen as completion of an emotional cycle or the culmination of a beautiful relationship. It feels final but joyful. However, the Tens are cards of transformation. In the Nine, we gained confidence and are near completion. In the Ten, we are crossing our final t's and dotting our final i's. We are starting a whole new cycle while we're finishing the current one. We are transforming. You cannot go through the One through Nine of any suit without being changed, and in the Ten of Cups we have been transformed by art, by beauty, by all kinds of love, by our own emotional journeys. We have transformed in how we want to express ourselves and what we want to express. It feels easy now, and still we might find difficulties we didn't expect. Nonetheless, we are no longer shy and timid when it comes to self-expression. We are ready to show the world who we've become. We are ready to create.

Getting to Know the Cups Suit

Pull out your Cups cards if you haven't yet and put them in order from One to Ten. From there, look through the keywords listed below, and note any personal associations you have with the card in the third column.

Card	Traditional Associations	Personal Associations
Ace of Cups	Associated with The Fool and The Pages Start of an emotional cycle Start of a relationship New ideas to express or create from Overflowing emotions	
Two of Cups	Balanced emotions A reciprocal relationship Putting our emotions into something more holistic Art that makes you whole	
Three of Cups	Party time! (a.k.a. Celebration) Working in groups or with others Friendship	

Card	Traditional Associations	Personal Associations
Four of Cups	Ennui Reevaluating Disconnection/disassociation Feeling out of sync Opportunity offered but it's all the same *or* you just don't see it	
Five of Cups	An ending A heartbreak Letting go A release	
Six of Cups	Nostalgia that can help or hinder The past Childlike attitudes, energy, and innocence	
Seven of Cups	Daydreaming Head in the clouds Overwhelmed by options, ideas, or emotions Wait until the dust settles to make a decision	
Eight of Cups	Bittersweet ending Embracing the unknown Leaving for a better time	
Nine of Cups	Wishes coming true/ manifestation Satisfaction and happiness It's safe to splurge or indulge	
Ten of Cups	Transformation via love, art, beauty, and the like Ultimate happiness, success, satisfaction Harmony and alignment	

A Court of Cups

When studying the tarot, we usually learn and teach the Court Cards first as versions or parts of ourselves. Since the Cups cards are so focused on expression and how that impacts our ability to care for ourselves and create, that is what we have reflected below.

The **Page of Cups** is that childlike version of ourselves that gets excited about the "silly" things we love and wants to run outside to play when springtime hits instead of staying in and working. In a reading aimed at creativity or self-expression, this card is likely telling you to let your playful side show through. Pepper some jokes into your writing. Play with asymmetry or "coloring outside of the lines" in your visual art. Do a bunch of improv games instead of jumping right into rehearsal for a Serious Performance Art Piece. Let that inner child come through and know your work will benefit from it.

The **Knight of Cups** matures pretty quickly. A romantic at heart, this is the version that shows up for our loved ones ready to fight for them. Yet this is also the side of ourselves that perpetually wonders what and who else is out there, even if we get upset with ourselves for feeling that way. In a reading about creativity or expressing ourselves, the Knight of Cups *wants* to focus on the beauty and the rose-colored glasses. What they *need* to do however is express all of the confusing emotions within themselves including conflicting desires or ideals.

The **Queen of Cups** is the master of emotions. Queens in general correlate to water, making the Queen of Cups "water of water." While this may sound overwhelming, this Queen is actually the mature version of ourselves who knows that our emotions are holy and deserve to be honored. When this Queen shows up in a reading for creativity or self-expression, they are reminding you that there is a healthy way to make or say what you want and that you'll be happier if you find that middle ground while still putting your whole emotional self into it.

This is a Queen that people rarely have trouble relating to The Empress. Self-care and happy indulgence? Check. Creations galore? Check. Mastery of the emotions and elements that got us here? Check. The trick here is in learning to differentiate them. The Queen of Cups is happy to settle into a balanced emotional routine full of love, art, and contentment. The Empress still wants us to strive for more, and it is through this face that she shows us what "more" can look like.

The **King of Cups** is the side of us that represents "peak" Cups energy. So this is the side of ourselves that is a little too sensitive sometimes. This is the part of us that wants to paint all day when actually we should hop online to sell some of our art instead. This side of ourselves *has* the prerequisite skills to be successful but wants nothing more than to escape into and drown in beauty, art, and personal relationships and to overindulge and under-deliver. Yet this King simply needs to be heard, and if we can harness this energy when it shows up in a reading about our creativity or self-expression, we can create our most authentic work yet.

Getting to Know the Cups Courts

Now it's time to figure out how *you* see the Cups Court Cards, and how that can help or hinder your ability to express yourself. If you get stuck or just want to repeat ideas outlined above, shuffle them as best you can and lay them out in a new order to see what pops up.

Card	Traditional Associations	Personal Associations
Page of Cups	Inner child Whimsy, play, imagination Curiosity Creative opportunities	
Knight of Cups	Romance and devotion Charm and beauty Artists and their creative work Rose colored glasses, naivety	

Card	Traditional Associations	Personal Associations
Queen of Cups	Mastery of emotions, emotional stability Intuition and empathy Compassion, care, and feeling synchronized with others Able to put feelings into all they create	
King of Cups	Diplomatic, empathetic, and understanding Emotional and sensitive Expresses deep emotions easily when they feel understood and heard	

Cups Court Cards Activities

Think about when you specifically connect to the ideas described above. Take some notes on the specific version of yourself that you see in your Court Cards or in the descriptions above.

Then, shuffle these Court Cards up (as best as you can shuffle four cards) and pull one. This card is telling you which version of yourself your creative soul is crying out for right now, which side of yourself is dying to be expressed.

Cups Self-Care Prompts

1. A **journaling prompt:** Literally just check in with your feelings. How ya doin' and why?

2. **Drink something cold or hot**, whichever would be soothing now. Really feel that liquid move down your throat and into your stomach.

3. **Check in with someone you love**, and specifically someone who always asks how you're doing once they answer your initial questions. Invite them to do something fulfilling and fun for both of you.

Cups Creative Prompts

1. **Beauty and the Cups:** Early on in this chapter we asked you to assess your interpretation and relationship to the Cups keyword "Beauty." After working through this chapter, write or visually create a reaction to that keyword.

2. **In your collaborator's eyes:** Imagine that a project you've been working on is a collaboration (or do this with an actual collaborative work). Pull a couple of cards and imagine this is your collaborator giving you feedback on your end of the project. What praise does this card give you? Where does this card feel like you fell short or like something isn't working? Where is there neutral feedback that might be ideas for editing or going deeper? The latter would be sentences that started with "What would happen if we . . . " or something like that. You can separate your Cups cards and do this with just those, but you can also use your whole deck. The readings will be in the spirit of Cups' relationships and collaborations, so using the whole deck will still have that effect.

3. **Ultimate fulfillment:** The Ten of Cups is one of the happiest and most joyful cards in the tarot deck. Pull yours out and study it. This is often brushed aside as a fluffy, happy card or like it's unrealistic but when you look at the Cups as a whole story you see it is a hard-won and hard-fought happiness. Think about where you are right now in a healing journey and what you're trying to heal from. Set a timer for 10 minutes and imagine getting to the end of this journey. What does it feel like? What does it look like? What does life, post-healing, look like for you? Now create a visual or written account of that time and keep it somewhere that is easy to spot and visualize with. This is both a creative and manifestation exercise.

Cups Card Spreads

Emotional Clarity Spread

This is a self-care spread for those times when our emotions are all muddled together. It can also be used in creativity when we're not sure what core mood or emotion we are going for.

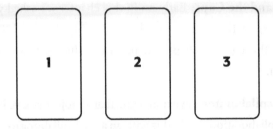

Card 1: What am I feeling right now?

Card 2: Why am I feeling this way?

Card 3: How can that be harnessed into something creative and tangible right now?

Self-Expression Spread

Similar to the above spread, this one is best used when the words are coming out wrong or when the focus of a conversation, activity, or art project feels "off" or inauthentic. It should cue you in to your own voice and empower you to move forward from that place.

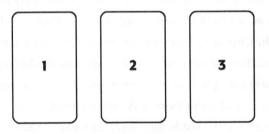

Card 1: What am I trying to say?

Card 2: Why is what I'm trying to say not coming out right?

Card 3: Is there a better way to express myself in this moment?

Making Beautiful Creative Work Spread

This tarot spread is pretty much what it sounds like—some areas of focus and thought and a couple of jumping off points for you to zoom in on and then zoom *out* on to create beautiful things.

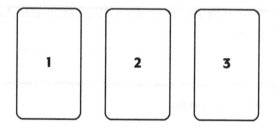

Card 1: A prompt for brainstorming for your creative work.

Card 2: What shape can the ideas in the first card take? In other words, what do the ideas I came up with in brainstorming look like as I move toward putting them in a creative project?

Card 3: Where can I incorporate something unique or beautiful to really make this creative work mine?

Cups Ritual:
Create a Self-Love Anointing Oil

Oils are one of our favorite ways of working with water magic. They can be used to anoint yourself or a candle for candle magic. You can anoint doorways with protection magic and pour them into your bath to soak up that magical energy. It is fairly easy to make your own anointing oils, and this one has been created by Siri for help with self-love.

The most important consideration when choosing herbs for your anointing oils is how they interact with your body. If you are allergic to a plant, you should absolutely not use that plant in your anointing oil! There are also some common essential oils that are not great for putting on your skin—cinnamon being one of those.

The ingredients that are listed below should be safe for your skin; however, please do make substitutions if you need to, so long as they are skin safe. Additionally, if you don't want to go out and buy extra materials, you can use kitchen herbs for this.

Materials:

- 2 parts dried rose petals

- 1 part dried lavender buds

- 1 part dried calendula flowers

- 1 part dried orange peel

- Jar

- A fine strainer or coffee filter

- Skin-safe oil: sweet almond oil, grapeseed oil, or olive oil are great options

Step One: Gather all of your ingredients. If you use only one herb in this oil, let that herb be rose petals! (You should be able to find dried rose petals fairly easily.) This recipe is purposefully written so that you can create any amount of anointing oil you want to create. Place the dried herbs in the jar. About one third of the jar should be left empty.

Step Two: Cover the herbs in your oil of choice. Fill the jar to the top, so that the oil is even with the lip of the jar. You don't want there to be much space left in the jar, because you don't want your oil to mold.

Step Three: Leave the jar alone for 4 to 5 weeks. For the first couple of days the oil is infusing, shake the jar to make sure there is an even-ish distribution of herbs.

Step Four: After 4 to 5 weeks have passed, you can strain the herbs out of your oil. Jar the oil in whatever jars you have (I recommend little jars with a dropper). You can use this as a perfume oil, an anointing oil, or any other way you want.

11

PENTACLES–CREATING A SUSTAINABLE PRACTICE

Pentacles are the rich soil for our roots to dig deep, nurturing and sustaining us.

The suit of Pentacles is extremely down-to-earth, even subtle at times. It takes time to get to know this suit. Pentacles are about cultivation, nurturing, and slow growth. They unfold before us like a late-blooming flower: a glorious gift. Their energy is subtle and beautiful. It takes time to get to know them and it is so very worthwhile.

Pentacles correlate to Earth, a magical element that also gets brushed aside until you realize how much witchcraft connects back to it. Stones, herbs, animals, your body—all of these are Earth element modalities. When we realize that, we get closer to what the Pentacles are trying to show us. This represents the materials that we use—the specific paint we prefer, the medium of our art, the incense that inspires us, the technology we use to create. It is so often the materials that get us to move from ideation and into creation. The materials we use help us to get our ideas out there, give our creations shape in the world. This is all Earth energy.

The element of Earth is magically connected to the processes of growth and abundance, while helping us build stability. Earth nurtures us, literally feeding us and providing shelter. In traditional Wicca, the element of Earth is represented on the altar with a Pentacle or a bowl of salt; many witches will actually use representations of Pentacle court card members on their altars to stand in for this element. The story of Pentacles is a gentle unfolding of our relationship with the Earth, and all that nature has to offer. The lessons in these cards help us connect to nature, build sustainable practices, and learn what abundance truly means for us.

Siri

The Pentacles suit is one that a lot of beginner tarot students deem boring. I know I did. It wasn't as flashy as the Wands, as mysterious as the Swords, or as romantic as the Cups. Not only that, but also, as someone who wasn't interested in capitalism, I had a lot of weird ideas about Pentacles and how they relate to money. However, this suit is far more than money, and the cards show us their many facets the longer we work with them. These cards move a little more slowly. They might not feel as exciting as the other suits, but they are absolutely necessary.

We have written throughout the course of this book that it's important not to see the cards as linear. Yes, they tell a story, but just because you pull the Two of Swords doesn't mean the Three of Swords is coming next. However, the suit of Pentacles is not quite like the other suits and often *does* feel linear. When you turn to the tarot to assess your own personal growth, you are looking to pinpoint where you are in the process. Sometimes we just want to understand what needs our attention at this moment and how we should plan for the future. So it can be really useful to look at this suit as a progression! Of course, tarot is not always predictive. You could make a decision that totally changes the progression, or you could be unhappy with the direction you're headed and start all over again. Knowing where you are in the process is the first step: from there, you always have the free will to choose.

Pentacles really live with the aphorism "what you pay attention to grows." It is the careful tending of a garden, planning for a better future. This suit is all about paying attention to the things that we want to increase in our lives and making gentle plans to make them happen. I think that a sense of comfort resides here, showing us the earthly things that are really necessary for our own lives and growth.

When I think about my creative life, I think of building worlds and new visions. Part of why I read so much science fiction, fantasy, and romance is because I want there to be a different kind of world. Writing my own fiction can get me into the mindset of building that world. It allows me to attempt to understand the complexities necessary for a better world for all of us, and that's absolutely beautiful. Then, the down-to-earth, slow, and steady pace of the Pentacles is really helpful. It means that we can translate this vision to reality—and take the time we need to get it right.

But unfortunately, we still live under capitalism, which means having a head for numbers, and money is essential. In recent years I've shifted away from thinking about it as purely money, and more into thinking about things in terms of resources. This has helped me tremendously in recognizing the abundance around me, even when I'm flat broke.

Learning how to use your resources is the key to creating and maintaining a creative career. The suit of Pentacles can help us get there in a sustainable way and help us learn to sustain ourselves.

While the other suits might bring in ideas and action quickly, the suit of Pentacles is all about the careful execution of those ideas.

In the Rider-Waite-Smith deck, The Empress is surrounded by a field of wheat, with water in the background. This shows their deep connection to earth and growth, and the sweetness of The Empress's message. The Empress is a riot of fertility, golden fields in the wind—the word "lush" springs to mind. This is a two-way support: just as The Empress supports us through nature, so too do we need to support nature through careful stewardship of our resources.

. . . .

Styles of witchcraft to play with: Plant magic, grounding, working with land spirits, magical herbalism, attraction magic, money magic, agricultural magic

. . . .

. . . .

Styles of creativity to play with: Cooking and baking, pottery, sculpture, fantasy world-building (emphasis on building)

. . . .

. . . .

Tarot cards that feature Earth: The Emperor, The Chariot, Strength, The World

. . . .

The Journey through the Pentacles

Stability and sustainability are the main themes of the Pentacles suit, and this means that the suit as a whole is filled with powerful allies for your personal self-care and creative journey. There is a stereotype of the creative person as being chaotic, as not having a stable foundation to draw from for their work. We've already debunked that, but the Pentacles show us how it's possible to be grounded, steady, dependable, *and* creative.

Here is where we think about methodology; here is where we perfect our craft. Pentacles are also a suit of legacy—and therefore they are of deep interest for people who are creative in their careers. Think of Nicole Kidman or Morgan Freeman: they have a wonderful history of work to look back on, they have had time in their lives to experiment, and they are able to take on their dream roles. This is also a time to incorporate play and joy into your work. As much as the Pentacles can be a suit of toil, they are also a curious, exploratory journey that can support us in seeking to learn about our craft.

Pentacles can be a pretty straightforward story—it has some twists and turns, but it is mostly a journey from one place to the other.

The **Ace of Pentacles** is the initial vision of stability that is cultivated through the rest of the suit. It holds fertile ground to grow and move and change. This is the initial planting of a seed that you can cultivate throughout the rest of your journey. Traditionally, this card represents an opportunity being offered to you. The Aces are a great place to start gathering the resources you need to make your dreams come alive. Gathering your resources is also investing in your work—investment being one of the keywords of this card. If you're a digital artist, this might mean upgrading your tablet. If you're a painter, it might mean keeping all of your paints at hand and resupplying when necessary instead of putting it off. This is supported by the idea that some tarot readers have of the Pentacles/Earth as materia. The Ace of Pentacles question for you is this: How can you continue to invest in yourself and your creative process as you near the end of this book?

The **Two of Pentacles** is our next step and represents multitasking and juggling many different commitments. Building off the energy of the Ace, this card is a lesson in getting specific with your projects and where you put your creative energy. It often shows a figure juggling two pentacles, and in the Rider-Waite-Smith deck it shows some ships withstanding tall waves in the background. This can represent a feeling of turbulence, as if things aren't in balance. The theme of this card is finding harmony amongst the chaos. You might feel pulled in multiple directions in the short term, but there is potential to find a balance. For creatives, this card represents projects that are being juggled. It's a sign that you need to choose something and really dedicate your creative time to working on that something, rather than dividing your energy and ultimately creating something mediocre. Remember: just because you choose a focus now doesn't mean that you can't work on other projects later.

Now that we have a specific vision, we need to find other people who can help us to realize that vision. The **Three of Pentacles** is about building something with your community. There's a strong theme of collaboration in this card.

If you had to make a decision in the Two of Pentacles about direction, the Three of Pentacles shows that you are moving forward steadily with the help of others. The Threes tend to be collaborative cards in the tarot and the Three of Pentacles can also represent everyone in the project knowing their role. Often this card depicts several people with different jobs all working toward the same goal. This is particularly important if your art is collaborative—such as in theatre or music. Even if your art is just you, this might be a sign that you're looking for a group to support and learn from. Taking a more monetary approach to this card, the Three of Pentacles could be a sign that you need to hire someone to help you, like someone to build your website.

When we think about the Three of Pentacles in connection with The Empress, we think about that lush garden, and how root systems are connected underground. If a garden is laid out well, the same water and nutrients feed everything, and each plant does its own thing. Yet on the surface, we see a beautiful merging of stunning flower displays and delicious herbs. It takes work to do this, and it takes trust in these underground systems to do their own thing. This Three pushes us to find our roots, our role, our specialty, and then sit back and enjoy that when together we all start flourishing.

The shadow side of the suit begins to come out with the **Four of Pentacles**. This often represents greed, hoarding materials, and fear of losing your wealth. The Four of Pentacles isn't usually a particularly pretty card and often shows a figure hoarding resources. Scarcity mindset can encourage an inspiration block when we are trying to create. It's important to tease apart the ideas of scarcity mindset and a true lack of funds. These feelings can often block you from thinking creatively about how to use the resources that *are* available to you. Scarcity mindset—present in this card—is the belief that there will never be enough, which results in fear, stress, and anxiety. Scarcity mindset doesn't always add up to the reality of your resources; very often, it is a trauma response to times in your life when there truly wasn't enough. Working with the energy of this card—and attempting to move through that energy—means knowing the difference between when you are in a trauma response vs. when you truly need to conserve resources.

The **Five of Pentacles** builds off of this energy and shows what it means to have true need rather than perceived need. In the Rider-Waite-Smith deck, we've gone from a king hoarding wealth to two people experiencing extreme poverty, wandering through the streets in winter. This is the societal consequence of that hoarding. When this card shows up it often means that there is truly a problem with resources. Yet there is some hope in this card— specifically it's a call for you to ask for help. We'll see the outcome of asking for help in the Six of Pentacles but for now it is something we are struggling to summon up the courage to do. When we think about the Five of Pentacles and creativity, we learn that it is hard to create when you don't have your material needs met. Yes, creativity can be a way of self-soothing in difficult times but more often than not, most people feel blocked and anxious when experiencing any level of poverty. It's okay to take a break to tend to yourself at this time. Your ideas will flow again.

The **Six of Pentacles** shows the redistribution of wealth that was so necessary in the Four and Five. In the Rider-Waite-Smith deck, the card features someone who appears wealthy to giving money to people who appear to be in need. It's nice to think of this card as resource redistribution, rather than charity. It is making the imbalance right again. Another keyword for this card is philanthropy. A lot of modern decks show this as more of a partnership, a give and take, rather than simply charity. In terms of our creative life, this could mean networking and figuring out the different needs in the community, or perhaps applying for and receiving grants for your creative work. There is also a strong sense of social justice in this card. From here on out, this suit is about building power and nurturing ourselves and our community, and all of that starts with realizing the disparities in our communities and building mutual aid and care. A part of that community care is sharing your creative pursuits with others—who knows, maybe other people read your stories or listen to your music as a form of self-care!

In the **Seven of Pentacles** we are finally seeing the fruits of our labor pop up. There is a moment to rest, and a moment to figure out where you want to go from here. Whether this is a card of harvest or of nurturing depends on your specific deck. Some decks show a person harvesting vegetables, and other decks show them paused and looking down at their work. Either way, this card is a powerful indication that the things that you focus on will in fact come to be. This card is about attention more than anything else. It raises the question, "What will you focus on?" For our creative lives, the Seven of Pentacles shows us that careful consideration and attention to what matters the most to us are essential. It also shows an ease that comes from pacing ourselves instead of running at breakneck speed toward our projects.

The pause in the Seven leads us into the **Eight of Pentacles,** allowing us to focus on craft and due diligence. The Rider-Waite-Smith deck shows a figure crafting a pentacle, with six other pentacles hanging up in their workspace and one below their workbench. This is a glimpse into the hard work that it takes to become a master of the craft. It is daily practice, diligence, and care—this is the best way to grow as an artist. Steady, daily practice makes perfect. This card is for daily writing challenges or completing a sketchbook filled with page-a-day sketches over the course of a year. This can also represent apprenticeship and learning from a master. Very often, building mastery is the next step once we have sorted out our physical self-care needs.

After every busy period we must take time to rest and to celebrate our accomplishments. The **Nine of Pentacles** is flamboyant, allowing us to blow off a little steam. This is a card of personal expression, as well as independence. You're allowed to expand and grow through all of this. You are allowed to celebrate your accomplishments. Your creative spark is not the same now as it was a year ago, or ten years ago. There's a sense of being in the present with the Nine of Pentacles, but also of looking forward to all of the beautiful things you want to create. This is a card that says it's okay to be a little flamboyant, that treating ourselves and gaining access to the finer things in life are essential. It's a good idea to surround yourself with beauty because it will continuously inspire you. It's also extremely important to enjoy your work, and a part of that is resting and building a personal haven.

We end on the **Ten of Pentacles,** rounding out our journey to abundance. This is a card that is not only about enjoying your work, but also about the creative legacy that you leave behind. When this card shows up, it tells us that our endeavors are supported in the long term, and we are able to build up our personal wealth and support our nearest and dearest while we do. It is the result of working slowly and consistently, building something beautiful over time. There is a sweetness to this card, an ending of a particular creative cycle that you are happy with. This makes me think of seeing my own work out in the world and being pleased with how it turned out. In terms of self-care, the Ten of Pentacles is all about being able to rest at the end of a productive cycle. Perhaps you've been busy working and creating, and now you need to take some time to savor the fruits of your labor.

Getting to Know the Pentacles Suit

As with the suits before, separate out your Pentacles from the rest of the deck. Lay them out in order and go through them. Check out the traditional association and elaborate on what they mean to you under personal association.

Card	Traditional Associations	Personal Associations
Ace of Pentacles	Offer Investment Financial gain	
Two of Pentacles	Multitasking Juggling commitments Prospects Possibilities	
Three of Pentacles	A good working group Collaborators Endorsement Recognition	

Card	Traditional Associations	Personal Associations
Four of Pentacles	Frugality Fear of financial loss Greed	
Five of Pentacles	Destitution Deprivation Hardships Ask for help	
Six of Pentacles	Philanthropy Charity Benevolence Resource redistribution	
Seven of Pentacles	Promotion Harvest Fiscal responsibility Pace yourself	
Eight of Pentacles	Apprenticeship Hard work Perfect your craft Aspiration	
Nine of Pentacles	Prosperity Refinement Independence Personal expression	
Ten of Pentacles	Stability Prestige Legacy	

A Court of Pentacles

The Pentacles Court is here to help us not only define our vision, but also figure out how to create sustainable systems for that work. They have both vision and skills that can assist you in sustaining yourself long term.

The **Page of Pentacles** is the part of ourselves that is deeply curious about systems and how to implement them. This Page is a perpetual student, always learning something new. This Page is not only concerned with how to do things, but they also want to do these things beautifully. When this energy is present in your life, you may find beauty in order and be extremely curious to see how things unfold. They have a knack for encountering the resources necessary to do what they would like, and they are also generous with the resources they encounter. Another way of reading the Pages is as a messenger, and in this instance a Page showing up in your reading could indicate that you are about to receive news about finances or resources needed to pursue your craft. In terms of creativity, this Page is interested in helping you hone your craft and learn from others to make your work stand out even more.

The **Knight of Pentacles** takes slow, deliberate action toward their goals. So often Knights are about action, and the Knight of Pentacles is the slowest of the group. This could perhaps be frustrating if you feel like you need to take action more quickly. However, this could be a good sign that what you actually need to do is slow down and consider all of the possibilities. The Knight of Pentacles is ultimately one of the most reliable Knights because they are incredibly stable and take action only when they feel completely ready. When the Knight of Pentacles shows up in a reading, it might mean that you need to channel some of their rationality. It could also mean that progress on your project will be slow, but that ultimately you will be pleased with the results.

The **Queen of Pentacles** is the master of our inner nurturance and personal sovereignty. They are charitable, noble, and extremely caring. When this Queen shows up for us, it's a sign that we need to treat ourselves deliciously. The Queen of Pentacles is often shown on a throne surrounded by plants and flowers, representing the fruits of their labor cultivated in a beautiful space. This is another card that speaks to the incredible generosity of The Empress. The wealth that they have cultivated is not just for themself, but for everyone. This Queen is a queen of inner sovereignty, and that is particularly important to consider because they are so very stable. This Queen has the stability necessary to really give of themself. If this card comes up in a reading, it is an opportunity to step into your own nurturance and grace around the material world.

We probably don't need to extrapolate too deeply on how this Queen connects back to The Empress. Let's look instead at how this Queen and The Empress are different. While the Queen of Pentacles rests easily and allows themself to indulge, it's not quite to the level of The Empress. A shadow side of this card might be a tendency to associate self-worth with how hard one works or how valuable one is to others through either material gifts or constant favors. The Empress has transcended this and knows their worth is simply in their gifts and experiences, whatever those might be. Where the Queen of Pentacles stands out is in the sheer amount they have achieved in whatever is important to them, and this tends to be a card linked to people in our life that we deeply respect.

The **King of Pentacles** is the outward ruler of the suit, meaning that they are in charge of materials for a group of people. This King is powerful, established, and resource-rich. This is someone who is capable and understands resource distribution. This King is extremely well versed in how to manage resources fairly, ensuring ease now and growth for the future. This is an absolutely necessary skill and can be the difference between an artistic endeavor succeeding or failing. Of course, we don't like to think about what would happen if we lose our funding, but planning for the future (and in some cases planning for the worst) is an essential part of long-term artistic work.

Getting to Know the Pentacles Court

Again, take out your Pentacles Court Cards and lay them out in front of you. Go through each card one by one and make any notes about them that you want to in the section below.

Card	Traditional Associations	Personal Associations
Page of Pentacles	Practical Stylish Scholarly Receipt of financial news	
Knight of Pentacles	Methodical Rational Stable Reliable	
Queen of Pentacles	Charitable Noble Opulence Nurturing	
King of Pentacles	Powerful Enterprising Established Practical leadership	

Pentacles Court Cards Activities

Pull out all of your Pentacles court cards and line them up. Go through each of the court cards and jot down any notes you have about them. How they make you feel, your assumptions about them as people, and what resources you find on the cards are all good places to start.

Which of these cards do you identify with the most? Which of these cards do you feel the farthest removed from? Think about what lessons your Pentacles Court Cards might have for you, specifically.

Court Activity: Choose Your Court

Now that we have gone through every suit, I wanted to share an activity that I love to do periodically. It's time to get to know your Court—the one that is specific to you. In this section, we will be looking at what energy best suits you at this time, the lessons you need to learn, and who your best allies are.

Take out all of the Court Cards from all of the suits. Line them up in whatever order makes most sense to you. Now, look at each "role" of the Court Cards (for example, Page as a student, Knight as action, and so forth).

1. Which Page best identifies how you are a student at this time?

2. Which Knight best identifies how you take action at this time?

3. Which Queen shows your mastery of self at this time?

4. Which King shows how you are a leader?

Write any additional notes. Feel free to come back to this activity fairly regularly, as your court might shift around as you grow and learn new lessons.

Pentacles Spreads

Creative Intentions Spread

As we move into the next phase of our creative journey, let's revisit some of the creative goals that you've set for yourself, and perhaps set new creative intentions. I use the word intention specifically. You cannot fail at an intention, there is no preconceived judgment of an intention. There is flexibility here for you to shift and move as you find ever more clarity in your creative process.

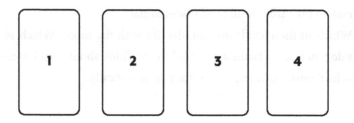

Card 1: What is your creative intention for this time?

Card 2: What do you need to know as you work toward your intention?

Card 3: What is the most logical next step?

Card 4: What is a daily action you can take to move toward your intention?

Creative Sustainability Spread

As you move into the next phase of your creative life, it's time to start thinking about what sustains you for long-term creativity. The Pentacles suit is a really good suit for building momentum and sustaining it long term, so this spread is supposed to help you do just that.

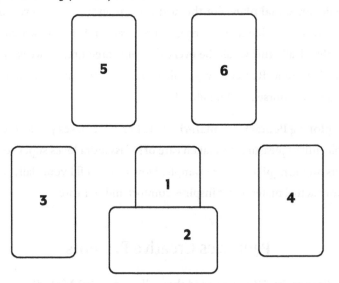

Card 1: You, as a creative at this moment

Card 2: What are the biggest challenges to your creativity?

Card 3: What is your most important resource for your creative process long term?

Card 4: How can you overcome your creative challenges in the long term?

Card 5: What routines or habits do you need to build?

Card 6: Anything else that helps

Pentacles Self-Care Prompts

1. **Ground into your body:** Take a second to focus on your breathing and really root into your body. Start by tuning in to your feet planted on the floor, and then move up to your ankles. How do they feel? Now move on to your shin, then your knees, and so on and so forth until you get to the crown of your head.

2. **Make an actual plan:** For the next three months, or whatever timeline sounds reasonable to you, engage in self-care and creative activities regularly. Ideally this would be every day, but three times a week is a great starting point. Remember—goals should be attainable. We don't want you to set yourself up for failure!

3. **Exploring Pentacles as materia:** What materia makes you feel comfortable, full of pleasure, and taken care of? Cassandra loves super soft blankets and firm pillows, for example. How can you fill your daily life with more actual materia that inspires comfort and self-care?

Pentacles Creative Prompts

1. **Collect rocks.** Were you a kid that collected rocks? Me too! Chances are you have a favorite. Go get your favorite rock and hold it. Take several deep breaths and just focus on the rock. What does it remind you of? What images come to mind? Write or sketch something based on that. You could also mix a beverage or cook something that looks like said rock.

2. **Find your creative home.** Take some time to ground and center. Gently bring your mind to focus on your breath, the rise and fall of your chest. Close your eyes, and begin to imagine a door in front of you. This door opens into your creative space—a studio, a home, an office, wherever you do most of your creating. Once you have the door clearly in your mind, open it up and take a look inside. What does it look like? How is it decorated? Is there anything that surprises you? Take a look around. Ask for anything that you don't have that you want in this space. When you come out of meditation, think about how you can mimic some of the qualities of your inner creative home in your actual home.

3. **Envision a home for the Court Cards.** If you are a visual artist, draw the home of one of the Court Cards. What would their home look like? Would there be food out on the table, ready for a dinner party? Or would it be austere? Modern decoration or classic? If you are not a visual artist, take a moment to describe the setting of one of the Court Cards' homes. Imagine that this is the first introduction to their home. Put as many details in as possible.

Pentacles Ritual: A Charm Bag for Getting Habits to Stick

Sometimes it can be difficult to get habits to stick. If you have had a hard time settling into routines, or if you often break your routines and habits, it might be difficult to envision yourself doing what you need to do. Sometimes, a bit of magic can help those things work for you.

I find that it's really helpful to have a physical object that you can work with to help you ground and center. This can be something that you carry with you throughout your day—or that you leave in a prominent place so that you will see it and be reminded of your commitment to self-care.

Materials:

- Pen and paper (for design)
- A stone of some kind (more about this below)
- A small drawstring bag
- Rosemary
- Sage
- Peppermint

Step One: First, if you haven't decided what kinds of sustainable self-care habits you want to work with, you will want to work through some of the prompts above. Once you have figured out what self-care habits would support you the most right now, choose one that you can start. Write it on the piece of paper. If it's a more in-depth habit, write the steps it takes you to perform the habit.

Step Two: Select a stone for the charm bag. There are many options for this. If you have found a stone on the banks of a river or the shore of a lake that you love, that is perfect for this spell. If you would like a little guidance, here are some grounding and creative stones to choose from: Ametrine, Bloodstone, Carnelian, Clear Quartz, Fluorite, Gold Tiger's Eye, Jasper.

If you don't know much about these stones, I recommend that you go to a local metaphysical store and look at them. Go for whatever stone makes you feel the best, then read the description later. We have also included some keywords for each stone in the Materia appendix (page 171).

Step Three: Imagine yourself going through the self-care routine that you want to set. Really take a moment to slow down and let yourself do that. How do you want to feel? What does your ideal day look like—with this routine as a part of it? Pick up each of the items that will go in your charm bag and hold them while you go through the thought of it in your mind. This includes asking the herbs for help with your focus.

Step Four: Put your charm bag together.

Step Five: Place the charm bag on your altar. Over the course of the week, every day you do the routine, add another pinch of the herbs to the bag. After the week is over, carry the charm bag with you or leave it near where you will do the habit. This will serve as a reminder to you to complete your rituals.

LESSONS FROM THE EMPRESS
-FINAL THOUGHTS

he Empress has been our guide through this process of self-rediscovery. Now we can take a breath, look back at the path we have walked with The Empress, and start to bring our tools for creative self-expression out into the world.

Self-discovery is not a linear process; it is never something that is fully accomplished. The Empress wants us to love and nourish ourselves as we get to know ourselves. Learning how to express yourself is the ultimate act of self-love. It's no coincidence that two queer writers produced this work. For us, queerness is an essential aspect of self-expression—and it is also something that we have had to nurture over time. It's not always easy to be queer, and learning how to take care of ourselves *is* a radical act. This *is* about identity, and learning how to nurture our particular needs. We hope that throughout this process, you have been able to dive even further into your own identity.

Your tarot deck will always be there as a resource to help you learn more about your own needs. We have explored the tarot in depth through this particular lens, giving you new ways of relating the cards back to your own creativity. The cards are a potent assistant to self-care, helping us to channel the answers to our questions.

The cards can also help you as you are planning your creative projects. If you're facing writer's block, try pulling a few cards to see the root of your block. Maybe you want to channel some of that big, archetypal energy we explored in the Major Arcana. Pull a specific card to rest on your desk as you write. Maybe you want to stoke the fires of new ideas with the Wands, or cut through the muck and find clarity with the Swords. Perhaps you need to find the emotional core of your piece of art with the Cups, or you need to get grounded with the Pentacles. Your deck will help you connect to these states and will be a hopefully lifelong ally in your self-care practice.

Because that's what it is: a self-care *practice*. The Empress knows that self-care is something that you nurture and grow over time. The Empress is no stranger to work, but they do not toil. They know that it's important to build care into every part of the process. The Empress is here to help us learn how to avoid burnout, and how to sustain us in the long run.

Now It's Your Turn to Review

It's time for us to go back through the lessons of the tarot as they relate to The Empress. As teachers, we like to allow for learning to be a nonlinear process. It's often in repetition and review that you make the most connections. So this section is for you to digest what you have read in this work. You can make several notes, you can work through these quickly, or you can ponder them over a longer period of time. This is really just a space for you to reflect on your own journey with The Empress and make note of any takeaways.

Major Arcana

- What archetypes were you working with at the beginning of this book, and which archetypes are you working with now?

- What was the most surprising takeaway from this chapter?

Wands

- What are some of your favorite ideas that came through in the course of reading this book?

- What was the most exciting takeaway from this chapter?

Swords

- What have you learned about processing difficult things? What self-care tools do you have when it feels like you've got nothing but swords?

- What was the most clarifying takeaway from this chapter?

Cups

- How can you nourish your intuitive self to take better care of yourself?

- What was the most emotional takeaway from this chapter?

Pentacles

- What does creative stability look like for you?

- What was the most grounding takeaway from this chapter?

The tarot spreads, rituals, and prompts are things you can do over and over again. If you chose one creative work to make progress on throughout reading this book, you may want to return to certain activities to help you in other areas of your life. We want to leave you with one more spread—this time to help you process the work you have done in reading this book.

Tarot Spread: Continuing Your Relationship with The Empress

This spread was designed to help you process the lessons of this book. Tarot readers often use terms like "I've been in a Tower year" as a shorthand for the primary energy of whatever they're going through; in working through this book, you have been going through an Empress season.

Make a cup of tea, coffee, or whatever your favorite drink is, and sit down with this to learn how to carry the lessons from The Empress forward into your life.

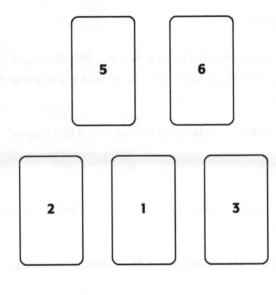

Card 1: You, now that you've finished this book

Card 2: Your most comforting lesson from The Empress

Card 3: Your most surprising lesson from The Empress

Card 4: Something to treasure

Card 5: Your creative direction

Card 6: A message from The Empress themself

Empress Final Ritual: Maintaining Our Lessons

In this ritual, you will celebrate the things that you have done over the course of this book to get to know yourself better, to find your own mode of self-expression.

This will be a ritual to help these lessons stick as you continue your tarot practice in a new way and solidify those self-care rituals you've developed over the course of this book.

Materials:

- A candle (this should ideally be a candle large enough to be lit every day for a month or two)

- The sigil you created in chapter 9

- Your Self-Love Anointing Oil created in chapter 10

- Your Habit Charm Bag created in chapter 11

- Your journal

- Your tarot deck

- Separate out the Queens from each suit and The Empress card

- A libation of your choice

Step One: Gather all of your materials, and ground and center.

Step Two: Visualize that a light is shining out from your heart. Everything this light touches is cleansed. As the light grows bigger and bigger, visualize it engulfing the area of your magical working.

Step Three: Now imagine that protective vines are coming out from the bottom of your feet, and that they slowly circle your working space. They coil upwards and upwards, until finally they have created a barrier between your inner light and whatever is outside of your working space.

Step Four: Turn to the East, Air, and place the Queen of Swords in that direction. Say aloud: "Queen of Swords, queen of boundaries and truth, I call you to this circle." If you see the directions as having different elemental correspondences, please feel free to use the ones you usually do.

Step Five: Turn to the South, Fire, and place the Queen of Wands in that direction. Say aloud: "Queen of Wands, queen of passion and creativity, I call you to this circle."

Step Six: Turn to the West, Water, and place the Queen of Cups in that direction. Say aloud: "Queen of Cups, queen of intuition and love, I call you to this circle."

Step Seven: Turn to the North, Earth, and place the Queen of Pentacles in that direction. Say aloud: "Queen of Pentacles, queen of nourishment and sustainability, I call you to this circle."

Step Eight: Turn to your main altar, and place The Empress card on it. Say aloud: "Empress, archetype of self-care, empowerment, and creativity, I call you to this circle!"

Step Nine: Take a moment to bask in the energy of these five archetypes all coming into the circle together. As you are feeling that energy, carve the sigil from chapter 9 into the candle. (A ballpoint pen works well for this.) Then, anoint the candle with the oil you created in chapter 10. Finally, place the charm bag from chapter 11 in front of the candle.

Step Ten: Light the candle.

Step Eleven: Take a while to journal through what your ideal day would be, if you were living the truest version of yourself. Start from the moment you wake up in the morning, to the moment you go to bed at night.

Step Twelve: If you feel so called, do a tarot reading for yourself. You can do the final Empress tarot spread from above.

Step Thirteen: Libation time! Celebrate yourself and pour that drink, eat that dessert, treat yourself!

Step Fourteen: Going in the opposite direction of setting the circle, thank The Empress and each of the Queens for their participation in the ritual. Then pick up all of your materials.

Step Fifteen: Over the next few months, light your candle in the morning. Take this as a moment to check in with yourself, your intuition, and your creative spirit. Let the lessons of The Empress wash over you. So mote it be.

MATERIA

You can make magic with anything and nothing. Materia—a.k.a. the materials that you use to cast—is there to help. The spells and rituals presented in this book are purposefully low on materials required. For those materials that are not already in your home, you can probably find them fairly easily at your local occult bookstore. You can even think of the search for these items as a part of your magic-making.

We highly recommend that everyone work with a grimoire or journal as a part of the work in this book. It's an important tool that you can use for recording your experience, and it will also be something you can come back to later. This can also just be in your regular journal or grimoire.

The following list of ritual correspondences for creativity is meant to help you enhance your magical and tarot practice throughout reading this book. If you are looking for things to put on your altar, you can use this list! You can also check this list to see if there are things you already have with you that you can utilize throughout this book.

Correspondences for Creativity

Planet: Jupiter, Mercury, Moon, Sun, and Venus

Color: Blue, Gold, Green, Orange, Purple, Silver, Yellow

Incense/Scent: Cinnamon, Honeysuckle, Jasmine, Patchouli, Sandalwood

Gemstones (see below for specific recommendations): Amethyst, Ametrine, Bloodstone, Carnelian, Citrine, Clear Quartz, Fluorite, Gold Tiger's Eye, Iolite, Jasper, Moonstone, Rose Quartz

Herbs: Broom, Cardamom, Carnation, Chamomile, Clove, Ginseng, Hawthorn, Lavender, Lilac, Lotus, Mistletoe, Orchids, Passionflower, Peppermint, Rose, Rosemary

Foods: Avocado, Apples, Cherries, Honey, Cake, Maple Syrup, Pomegranate

Deities and Spirits: Aengus, Apollo, Astarte, Athena, Baldr, Bragi, Brigid, Cerridwen, Coyote, Dionysus, Ea, Enki, Eros, Fae/Fairies, the Fates, Hephaestus, Jupiter, Kali, Lakshmi, Lugh, Maia, Mercury, Mimir, Minerva, Prometheus, Ptath, Rhiannon, Sarasvati, Seshat, Taliesin, Thoth, Vulcan

Looking at this list, is there anything you disagree with? Is there anything that you absolutely love? Make your own correspondence list below!

Correspondences for The Empress Tarot Card

The Empress also has their own list of correspondences. There are things that tarot readers, artists, and creators have associated with this tarot card over the centuries, and so any of these materials might also be great things to engage with this card specifically.

Planet: Venus

Zodiac: Libra, Taurus

Color: Green, Peridot, Rose

Incense/Scent: Amber, Rose, Sandalwood

Gemstones: Emerald, Rose Quartz, Turquoise

Herbs: Clover, Damiana, Rose

Foods: Cake, Corn, Honey, Root Vegetables, Wheat

Deities and Spirits: Ashera, Astarte, Baldr, Brigid, Cerridwen, Danu, Dôn, Freyja, Frigg, Great Goddess of Antiquity, Hera, Inanna, Isis, Juno, Jupiter, Lakshmi, Nut, Sarasvati, Venus

We also wanted to make sure that you are prepared for all of the rituals in this book. We've purposely kept the materials for the rituals fairly easy to find, but if you want to be extra prepared, here is a complete list of suggested materia from the rituals in this book:

- Your tarot deck

- Several candles—treat yourself and stock up!

- A feather

- A light bulb

- Dried rose petals

- Dried lavender buds

- Dried calendula flowers

- Dried orange peel

- Jar

- A fine strainer or coffee filter

- Skin-safe oil: Sweet almond oil, grapeseed oil, or olive oil are great options

- A stone of some kind

- A small drawstring bag

- Rosemary

- Sage

- Peppermint

There are many places that you can mix and match ingredients. We've tried to keep the rituals as cost-friendly as possible, though for the Cups ritual we did include some herbs that aren't standard kitchen herbs.

But just in case you are allergic or can't find the herbs listed above, here is a chart to help you understand why we chose these herbs and some potential alternatives:

Herbs Used in This Book's Rituals

Herb	Correspondences	Suitable Replacements
Rose	Attraction, love, blessings, beginnings, dedication, devotion, family, fertility, healing	Calendula, Jasmine
Lavender	Lunar magic, Mercury, communication	Jasmine
Calendula	Solar magic, beauty, attraction, divination	Rose, Sunflower, Marigold
Dried Orange Peel	Energizing, cleansing, beautifying, simplifying	Any other dried citrus peel, like lemon or grapefruit
Rosemary	Memory, ancestors, clarity, nurturing	Peppermint
Sage	Clarity, cleansing, safety, protection	Lavender, Cedar, Juniper
Peppermint	Memory, energy, clarity	Rosemary

Crystals for Creativity

When selecting things like crystals for use in creativity, it's a good idea to look at the other correspondences in the crystal. This can help you choose the right thing for your project. For example, if you are working on a poetry collection about the death of your father, you might want to choose a stone like Amethyst, which can also help you with grief and loss. However, if you're writing a rom-com, you might want to use something like Rose Quartz—which is all about the love!

Crystal	Associations
Amethyst	Supports creativity through emotional centering and intuitive decision making; protective and tranquilizing; helps make decisions; balances highs and lows; promotes emotional centering; dispels anger, fear, rage, and anxiety; supports during loss and grief
Ametrine	Helps creativity through having both mental and spiritual clarity about what you want to create, as well as the self-esteem to put your work out there. Combines power of amethyst and citrine; promotes prosperity; improves self-esteem; facilitates connection with higher consciousness; enhances spiritual and mental clarity; cleanses the aura; releases negativity
Bloodstone	This stone helps you to open up to creative projects that are grounding and nurturing. Supports grounding; opens the heart; promotes development of personal power; enhances courage; releases fear; fosters strength of mind
Carnelian	This is a great stone for restoring your energy and breaking through creative blocks. Grounds and anchors in reality; stabilizing; restores vitality and motivation; cleanses other stones; helps you accept the cycle of life; gives courage and promotes positive life choices; motivates for success

Crystal	Associations
Citrine	Citrine is a sweet stone for creativity and abundance; this is particularly good for people who make their living as creatives. Fosters self-esteem; promotes prosperity and abundance; enhances creativity; transforms negative energy to positive; encourages generosity; protects against self-destructive tendencies
Clear Quartz	Clear Quartz is a stone that adapts to almost any purpose. It is particularly good for finding clarity of message and clearing your mind. Powerful energy amplifier; absorbs, stores, releases, and regulates energy; raises energy to highest level; enhances psychic abilities; attunes you to your spiritual purpose
Fluorite	Fluorite is a fantastic stone to promote creativity in group settings. Protective on a psychic level; great for overcoming disorganization; grounding; heightens intuitive powers; brings stability to groups; increases confidence and helps with learning
Gold Tiger's Eye	This stone helps to energize you and point your creativity in the right direction. Combines Earth and Sun energies; enhances psychic abilities; protective; shows correct use of power; assists in accomplishing goals; helps if you're spaced out or uncommitted; useful for recognizing your and others' needs
Iolite	This is a good stone to spark inspiration—particularly good if you've been going through a dry spell, creatively speaking. Amplifies or encourages psychic insight; eases addiction; increases focus; tunes in to guidance from your higher self or higher beings; sparks inspiration

Crystal	Associations
Jasper	Helps you to have courage to create, even when times are stressful.
	Supreme nurturer; sustains and supports during stressful times; brings tranquility; facilitates dream recall; absorbs negative energy; brings courage; supports in conflict
	I highly recommend ocean jasper for the creativity aspects, and red jasper for grounding.
Rose Quartz	Rose Quartz is the perfect stone for self-care, so if your creativity needs a boost of self-care, this stone will work.
	Promotes and strengthens all types of love; fosters unconditional love; promotes joy; promotes emotional healing; fosters faith; strengthens hope; helps overcome despair; instills calm and peacefulness

CREATIVE APPROACHES TO THE TAROT

T here is so much we could write about tarot and creativity through the lens of self-care and creative growth, and through the lens of The Empress. This appendix takes your tarot practice a bit further by showing you various creative ways to approach the cards and unlock even more self-growth and self-expression.

Brainstorming

We've all heard of brainstorming. The kind of brainstorming that we're specifically talking about here is focused on generating the best ideas quickly and making a decision that you feel comfortable with and that you are *excited* to follow through on. Not all ideas are created equal, and there will be some ideas that you are willing to throw out. I find that usually the first idea I have during a brainstorming session is the worst idea I come up with in that session, so let yourself have "bad ideas."

Sometimes the issue you're trying to resolve is stuck in your brain. Maybe you've been trying to resolve the issue for a long time, and you're struggling to get past it. In this case, we find that sometimes doing a 5-minute round of brainstorming on a completely different topic—even a different project—is the best thing you can do. Then, once your brain has had sufficient time away, you can turn your mind to the real question at hand. That isn't a waste of your time—rather, it helps you get past some brain blocks.

There are several different ways to structure a brainstorming session, but usually you are attempting to answer a question or solve a problem. So when you're writing and you come up against a thorny issue, don't just try to write around it. Stop and start brainstorming. Then, when you return to the project, you'll have a much better idea of where you're going and will feel more confident about your direction.

Try each of our brainstorming techniques for yourself and see which ones work best for you.

Magic Questions

Magic questions help us focus our brainstorming sessions. I also think that it's important to give yourself time and space for your brainstorming. I like to set a timer for 5 minutes, minimum, when I am brainstorming for my novel.

Magic questions are the questions that you use to focus your brainstorming session. This is the question or problem you are attempting to solve. The way you ask this question is important—you don't just want quick and easy answers, you want the *right* answers.

So instead of asking:

"What kind of family does my main character have?"

You can ask questions like:

"What is the most supportive family my main character could have?"

"What is the most interesting family my main character could have?"

"What is the most unexpected relationship my main character could have with her twin sister?"

See the difference? You are getting more specific with the kind of solution you want, and at the same time sending a message to your brain that whatever ideas you come up with have to be *supportive, interesting,* or *unexpected.* The way we formulate language changes our entire perspective on the question. If one of those magic questions isn't working, stop your brainstorming session and make a new one. Sometimes what *isn't* working is the information you're supposed to get from brainstorming. Once you've figured that out, you can try to figure out what *is* working.

So how do you write a magic question?

Think about the problem you're trying to solve and think about what kind of answer you're looking for. From the above example, the problem is what kind of family to give the main character. The magic questions, "the most interesting family" or "the most supportive family" are the kinds of answers you're looking for.

Now: Try it for yourself. Choose a theme to brainstorm around and choose several different kinds of answers you're looking for surrounding that theme. Brainstorm for 5 minutes on each question, to see how it feels.

Mind Mapping

This is another one of those brainstorming processes that you have likely already done. The short explanation is that you choose the magic question and write it in the middle of a blank sheet of paper. Then, you set a timer (I usually go for 15 minutes at a time) and start to brainstorm. You can connect ideas to the main circle, or ideas can branch off of one another.

I find that mind mapping is a really good technique particularly when there are a lot of moving parts to the problem you're trying to solve. So, for example, when I'm trying to figure out a moment in the plot of my novel and there are several different characters involved, I might want to do mind mapping so that I could brainstorm the reactions of all of the characters at once. If I feel like focusing on one character at a time that's fine, too.

Of course, like the brainstorming technique above, the question that you ask matters. If it's not a question that you feel compelled by, or if the question seems to keep generating really simple solutions that don't help you, change the wording of the question.

Here are some more techniques to take your mind mapping to the next level:

- Color-code your ideas—take some markers or highlighters when you're done with your mind map, and assign meaning to the different colors. You could color-code it to different characters, or perhaps "good-fine-bad."

- If you're struggling to come up with something, keep your pen moving. Doodle, write nonsense at the bottom of the page, but keep the pen moving. That will keep your brain somewhat focused on the project at hand, even though you're feeling a little stuck.

- Do opposing mind maps! Say you are trying to figure out a series of challenges your main character needs to face. Open to two blank pages in your notebook, and on one page write, "What are the most interesting challenges this character could face?" and then on the next page, write, "Of those interesting challenges, which are the least interesting?" See what happens!

Fifty Ideas in 15 Minutes

Cassandra read about this tarot technique in Mark McElroy's *Putting the Tarot to Work,* which is a surprisingly fun book about using the tarot for business purposes. In it, McElroy suggests this activity as a group brainstorming activity in office settings.

As someone who primarily works for themselves and is blessed enough to have at least half of their income come from creative work, they've modified it just barely to suit their own purposes. For this you need a deck of cards, a timer set to 15 minutes, and some pen and paper or a blank computer document. From there, you pull a card and just start writing ideas based off of the tarot card. This could be based on the ideas in the art or by allowing chain-of-thought reactions from keywords to spill out. For example, if it's a Rider-Waite-Smith Four of Wands you might say "put up poles," "use three collaborators," or anything else that stands up visually. You might say "add some movement" if you're working on a piece of performance art or visual art based on the common interpretation of the card. Once you feel "tapped out" or blank for that card, pull another one and do the same thing. Keep going until your 15 minutes are up. This is supposed to move really quickly, so while you shouldn't beat yourself up for not hitting fifty, you should strive for that. I've gotten as few as thirty and as many as two hundred, so it really does range. Once you have your "fifty" ideas, you can go through and note the ideas that really stand out as being for you, for this project. Often I've accidentally brainstormed for future projects too, so I pull up a Google Doc I've labeled "Backburner" and add those there. I also have a document of "Active Projects" where some of my fifty ideas might come in more handy than the one I sat down to work on that day.

Improv, Embodiment, and Tarot

Cassandra, here. I have always loved improv in spite of so many of the stereotypes of bad improv being true. I learned so much about creativity by training in improv at HUGE Theater here in Minneapolis. I also learned things that I've used in *other* creative outlets as well as my tarot practice, so yes, the nerdy theatre kid is here asking you to bear with them for a moment.

Improv is most often used to describe a type of comedic theatre where there's no script, just a bunch of (hopefully) hilarious actors riffing off of each other. It does have a specific set of rules, the most famous being "Yes, and." This means that to do good improv, you need to support your scene partners by agreeing with whatever their character says, then adding to it. A scene falls flat fast if your scene partner says, "Oooh, I wonder what's good in the cafeteria," and you say, "What cafeteria? We're in a spaceship." That's not only disrespectful but also the audience immediately cringes. A better response if you really want or need to be on a spaceship for a scene is "Hopefully something better than the Earth food they served us yesterday!"

The improv rules are all centered around concepts that make great creative work regardless of field. They basically come down to "Give the audience as much information as possible, but make it fun" and "Learn to play nice with the others." Improv happens in all fields too. It might be called *freestyle* or *improvisation*, but there is improvised music, storytelling, and dance. The same basic rules and principles hold true there. You should improvise only to add something great to a piece.

I learned about embodiment as a tarot exercise in Mary K. Greer's *21 Ways to Read A Tarot Card*. Embodiment simply means taking an idea and processing it fully, to the extent of experiencing it fully "in your body." This can mean fully taking on and internalizing a deity, tarot card, or ideal. For this activity we just mean pulling a card and then adopting the position of a central figure on the card to tap into how the body feels in that position. Does it make you feel stately and regal, kind of sad and bored, or excited to be out in the world? Each of the cards will make you feel something if you give yourself over to this exercise, and it's a great way to deepen your understanding of the emotions and lessons of a tarot card. It's also a brilliant jumping-off point for creative exploration.

Using a combination of improv and embodiment can help you uncover new things about whatever it is you are creating or perhaps inspire new ideas. I suggest starting with a simple embodiment exercise. Pull a tarot card and embody that central figure, even if the central figure is a tree or a falling tower. Obviously don't hurt yourself if you're a chronic pain babe like myself, but get as close as your body will get without pain. Take a second to really feel and be in this moment.

Then . . . move. Where do you go from there? What is the natural course of movement or action to take? Do whatever your body or creative mind is pulling you to (safely) do. When you run low on steam or ideas, stop.

I've also pulled more than one card and improvised how I get from one card to the next physically, pausing to embody the next card when I get there. You can use speech, music, and the like in what you're doing, so don't feel shoehorned into mime, though you can certainly mime if you want to. Have a conversation with yourself, with a god, or with another character as you do this. Tell the story of what you're doing while you're doing it. Dance it out. Sing a song to imaginary woodland creatures. The point is to *improvise* and *embody*; so as long as you're doing that, you're doing great.

What just happened? Take a few notes about it. Write it down. Sit with it. See how it feels to start a new piece or fold what you just experienced into an existing one. Alternatively, this may have simply gotten your mind and body prepared to create. You might surprise yourself by simply jumping into a project, mind and heart free to explore new creative terrain.

Stage Cards

While a lot of this book is about moving beyond the tired, often stagnant common and traditional interpretations of the tarot, there's one tidbit about the cards that somehow has gotten lost over time. That is the idea of stage cards. Stage cards are tarot cards that look like they are taking place on a stage, as if the figures pictured are actors performing instead of figures fully immersed in their cards and the living of their lives. This likely *did* start with Pamela Colman Smith and the creation of the Rider-Waite-Smith deck. Smith was a stage actor, and this deck shows a couple of cards with a clear delineation (if you're looking for it) between the "playing space" and the actual landscape of the card. The Two of Pentacles in the Rider-Waite-Smith is a clear example of this, with the landscape well in the background of the card and the main figure juggling, presumably for an audience. The Ten of Cups is another example of this, but interestingly enough seems to be a still from behind the "actors," perhaps during curtain call.

It's easy to say that these cards are created this way because they denote an act or illusion, but I respectfully disagree. I think these cards connect back to the idea that "All the world's a stage, and all its men and women merely players" (this common adage is actually a quote from *As You Like It* by William Shakespeare) and challenge us to think about what we're presenting to the world using that Shakespearean framework. Professor Jeremy Fiebig taught me basically three-fifths of everything I know about Shakespeare during my time at Waldorf College. One of the things he taught us is Shakespearean Original Practices, which includes the idea that during Shakespeare's time there was not the heavy focus on realism that most plays, film, and even television hammer home now. Instead, everyone knew they were at a play. Everyone knew it was an illusion. The audience became a part of it. Even the boring Shakespearean histories (no offense, Shakespeare) were events full of conviviality and community. They were downright raucous some nights, with the actors and stagehands encouraging this. All of these ideas are present in these stage cards if you look for them.

Part of why the stage cards aren't talked about much now is likely because deck creators don't use this device as often, but sometimes they do and it's easy to miss! Look through your cards and see if anything strikes you as being staged or taking place on a stage. What does that tell you about the card and your interpretation of it? As you move forward into your own process, what does this tell you about the self or creating?

If the artist did *not* include these depictions, that's okay. Pull out your cards and see if there's justification for this line of thought anyway. If not, play with your cards for a minute and pretend there is. What does the stage version of this card's messages show you that the card, read more straightforwardly, may not? For deeper, more emotional self-care purposes as well as creative purposes, think about what this delineation means and how you can best express it moving forward.

Taroetry

Taroetry is a word I heard at a party writer Alex Franzen once threw. She used it to describe creating poems using tarot cards. You don't have to be a good poet or even have ever written a poem before to do these prompts. You don't even really have to like poetry. These exercises are about inspiration and creativity, period. You also don't ever have to show anyone this work. Curiosity and experimentation are good, actually, so even if you're not a poet, give some of these a try. Taroetry is both a great way to learn tarot and a way to just do something. Below are some examples of prompts we have used for this.

The method I use most often for taroetry is the **wordbanking** method. Pick five to ten words from your tarot card, and write whatever poem comes to your mind from that but highlights the words from your wordbank.

Acrostic Poems!

These are so silly and, as a self-proclaimed bad poet and diehard poetry lover, I think I've read three genuinely good ones that weren't specifically comedy. (There are actually a bunch of good acrostic poems in the comedy genre.) Yours can be serious or not and can definitely be bad. An acrostic poem is a poem where every line starts with the letter of a word that is the overall theme of the poem. You might remember doing a version of this with your name in elementary school, using adjectives to describe yourself instead of poetry lines beside each letter of your name.

One way to do an acrostic poem is to simply use the name of the card with each letter of that name being the starting letter for the line of a poem. So with the Death card, your first line would start with D. The second would start with E, the third with A, and so on. You can use the theme or message of the card in this method or not. Up to you.

Another method for a longer card name like the Seven of Pentacles would be to use a keyword you like for an acrostic. I read this card to mean the planting of new seeds in an arena you're already well versed in, so I might pick "Planting" or "Seeds" for my acrostic.

Party for One

I've learned a version of this prompt in improv, in poetry classes, and through both tarot and party games with friends. In those versions, you do one line of a poem or story, and then the next person does the next line, and it moves through the group like that. For this prompt, we'll modify the exercise I initially learned taroetry from and make it easy and fun for one person.

Take a deep breath and think about what you're going through in your life right now. Shuffle your tarot deck. Then, pull a single card off the top of the deck. Write a single line of a poem about it. Do this quickly. Don't overthink it. It can be based on the card's meaning, the art (which still ties in to the meaning), and your intuitive reaction. Pull a second card off the deck, and write a second line of a poem in the same way. Keep going until you feel done or you're out of paper, whichever comes first.

Haikus!

We'll end on a super-easy, fast, fun one! Tarot haikus! A haiku is a Japanese poem consisting of three lines. The first line has five syllables. The second line has seven syllables. The third (and final) line has five syllables. Traditionally there should also be a seasonal reference (called a *kigo*) though in modern day the seasonal reference is often missing. I really like it, though, so for an extra challenge do try to include it in some of your tarot haikus.

As an example, if I wrote a haiku about my day or mood on any given day in any given August it might go something like:

Pumpkin spice creamer/
Finally in my coffee/
Fall might really come.

To write your tarot haikus you can either:

- Pull one card and write a haiku based on your understanding of it

OR

- Pull three cards. Write the first line about the first card, the second line about the second card, and the third line about the third card. This is a more challenging haiku method because you do still want it to be a cohesive poem.

BIBLIOGRAPHY

Tarot and Witchcraft

Amberstone, Wald, and Ruth Ann Amberstone. *Tarot Tips*. Woodbury, MN: Llewellyn Publications, December 2003.

Crispin, Jessa. *The Creative Tarot*. Miami, FL: Atria Publishing, February 2016.

Frazier, Karen. *Crystals for Healing: The Complete Reference Guide*. Berkeley, CA: Althea Press, November 2015.

Greer, Mary K. *21 Ways to Read a Tarot Card*. Woodbury, MN: Llewellyn Publications, May 2006.

Krans, Kim. *The Wild Unknown Archetypes Deck and Guidebook*. San Francisco: HarperOne, October 2019.

Lipp, Deborah. *The Way of Four Spellbook: Working Magic with the Elements*. Woodbury, MN: Llewellyn Publications, April 2006.

McElroy, Mark. *Putting the Tarot to Work: Creative Problem Solving, Effective Decision Making, and Personal Career Planning*. Woodbury, MN: Llewellyn Publications, February 2004.

Miro, Shaheen, and Theresa Reed. *Tarot for Troubled Times: Confront Your Shadow, Heal Your Self, and Transform the World*. Newburyport, MA: Weiser Publishing, July 2019.

Moore, Barbara. *Tarot Spreads: Layouts and Techniques to Empower Your Readings*. Woodbury, MN: Llewellyn Publishing, April 2012.

Pollack, Rachel. *Seventy-Eight Degrees of Wisdom: A Book of Tarot*. Newburyport, MA: Weiser Publishing, September 2009.

Reed, Theresa. *Tarot: No Questions Asked: Mastering the Art of Intuitive Reading.* Newburyport, MA: Weiser Publishing, September 2020.

Snow, Cassandra. *Queering the Tarot.* Newburyport, MA: Weiser Books, May 2019.

Stephen, Rachael. "bright ideas spell: for story solutions and creative blocks," YouTube Video, 38 min, December 20, 2019, *www.youtube.com.*

Suzuki, Shunryu. *Zen Mind, Beginner's Mind.* Boulder, CO: Shambhala Publications, 1970.

Taylor, Hannah. "What Is Dan Harmon's Story Cycle? And How to Use It (with examples)." *Industrial Scripts,* October 8, 2018, *www.industrial scripts.com.*

Tea, Michelle. *Modern Tarot: Connecting with Your Higher Self through the Wisdom of the Cards.* San Francisco: HarperOne, June 2017.

Vesta, Lara Veleda. *Wild Soul Runes: Reawakening the Ancestral Feminine.* Newburyport, MA: Weiser Books, May 2021.

Wen, Benebell. *Holistic Tarot: An Integrative Approach to Using Tarot for Personal Growth.* Woodbury, MN: Llewellyn Publications, January 2015.

Creativity and Self-Care

Cameron, Julia. *The Artist's Way: 25th Anniversary Edition.* New York: Tarcher-Perigee, October 2016.

Campbell, Joseph. *The Hero with a Thousand Faces (The Collected Works of Joseph Campbell).* San Francisco: New World Library, Third Edition, July 2008.

Carding, Emily. *So Potent Art: The Magic of Shakespeare.* Woodbury, MN: Llewellyn Publications, July 2021.

Catmull, Ed. *Creativity, Inc.: Overcoming the Unseen Forces That Stand in the Way of True Inspiration.* New York: Random House, April 2014.

Chabon, Michael. *Maps and Legends: Reading and Writing along the Borderlands.* New York: Open Road Media, December 2011.

De Bono, Edward. *Six Thinking Hats.* New York: Back Bay Books, August 1999.

Des Barres, Pamela. *Let It Bleed: How to Write a Rockin' Memoir.* New York: TarcherPerigee, April 2017.

Grace, Marlee. *How to Not Always Be Working: A Toolkit for Creativity and Radical Self-Care.* New York: Morrow Gift, October 2018.

Nakamura, R. "How 'Will and Grace' Had a Real-Life Political Impact on Marriage Equality." *TheWrap,* September 28, 2017. *www.thewrap .com.*

Oliver, Mary. *Devotions: The Selected Poems of Mary Oliver.* Westminster, London: Penguin Publishing Group, November 2020.

Pickens, Beth. *Your Art Will Save Your Life.* New York: The Feminist Press at CUNY, April 2018.

Poehler, Amy. *Yes, Please.* New York: Dey Street Books, September 2015.

Salesses, Matthew. *Craft in the Real World: Rethinking Fiction Writing and Workshopping.* Berkeley, CA: Catapult Publishing, January 2021.

Smith, Patti. *Just Kids.* New York: Ecco Press, November 2010.

Tarot Decks Cited

Crowley, Aleister. *Thoth Tarot Deck.* Stamford, CT: U.S. Games Systems, 1969.

Gnaccolini, Paola. *Sola Busca Tarot: Museum Quality Kit.* Woodbury, MN: Llewellyn Publications, 2019.

Madenié, Pierre, Anna Maria Morsuci, and Mattio Ottolini. *Marseille Tarot: Professional Edition.* Woodbury, MN: Llewellyn Publications, August 2019.

McCloud, Cedar. *The Numinous Tarot.* Numinous Spirit Press, 2017.

Road, Christy C. *Next World Tarot.* San Francisco: Silver Sprocket, February, 2019.

Slow Holler Tarot collective. *Slow Holler Tarot.* North Carolina: Slow Holler, 2018.

Waite, Arthur Edward, and Pamela Colman Smith. *Smith-Waite Tarot Deck: Centennial Edition.* Stamford, CT: U.S. Games Systems, 2009.

ACKNOWLEDGMENTS

Our Shared Acknowledgments

We first want to acknowledge together the role that the attendees for our workshop *Creating in Wyrd Times* had in creating this book. Your creative ingenuity and compassionate feedback helped us make this book what it has become.

We also want to thank our Occult Writer's Group for all of the obvious reasons, but also for holding space and nurturing us as people first and then as writers.

We want to give a wholehearted thank you to Lisa Marie Basile for her incredible foreword and ongoing support of our work. We're so glad to have you be such a crucial part of this book.

We want to thank Thraicie Hawkner and the staff at The Eye, Lacey Prpić Hedtke and the staff at The Future, as well as the staff of Magus Books and Herbs for providing one or both of us with so many opportunities and continuing to have faith in us and our works.

We want to thank the podcasters, blog writers, and social media personalities who have interviewed both of us and helped us grow our platforms. Your work in the field is so necessary and we are grateful to be a part of it.

The Northern Lights Witch discord server—we owe you a debt of gratitude for how gracious and generous you are with your support of us, as well as how many ideas you've provided necessary feedback on.

Finally, we want to thank everyone at Weiser Books for this opportunity and for helping make this book as good as it can possibly be and reach as many people as it can possibly reach. We especially want to thank Kathryn Sky-Peck for everything she is and does and for taking a chance on our off-the-beaten-path book.

Siri's Acknowledgments

First and foremost, I want to thank Cassandra for being such an incredible collaborator! We've done a lot of collaborations in the past, and it has felt very special and good that this would move from a workbook for a class to a book-book for the masses. I am especially thankful for their experience and knowledge in navigating the publishing process. I couldn't have asked for a better collaborator on my first book.

Thank you so much to Anaïs, my spouse, my love. Thank you for putting up with me as I freaked out about the book, as I scrambled to finish this draft, as I doubted myself. You have held me through it all and are the best life partner I could ask for. Endless gratitude to you. Thank you for inspiring me to keep going with the proud sparkle in your eyes.

I want to thank my parents, Joe and Lavonne, for their constant support. They raised me to be the free-thinking, book-obsessed, creative person I am today. Thank you for allowing my dreams to flourish, thank you for creating a safe space for me growing up and always.

Thank you to all of my Patreon supporters, students, clients, and other folks who support my business. Without you, I would not have been able to write this book. Quite literally. I am so grateful to have so many supporters that allow me to do this kind of work and writing.

Thank you to Max, Chris, Hilary, Nate, Manny, Stevie, Maddy, Lacey, SJ, and the rest of my friends for your support! Thank you so much for making me laugh when I get too in my head, and for helping me keep it weird. Lord knows there's not enough joy in the world, and you help me keep it going.

Thank you to my spiritual mentor, Kari Tauring, for helping me stay in stav even in the midst of a pandemic. You are so generous and so wise and I am privileged to know you. Thank you to Johannes Gårdbäck, for your teachings on folk magic. You both greatly influenced the ritual sections of this book!

And finally, I want to thank you, dear reader. I am so honored that you would spend your time reading this work.

Cassandra's Acknowledgments

I obviously wanna thank Siri for taking this journey with me! This went from yet another weird idea I thought would be fun to do together to class materials to a full-fledged book. Best witches, forever. Also a huge shout out to Anaïs who bought us ice cream cake to celebrate this book and is always here cheering on our weird friendship and everything else xe can find to cheer on. I love you both so, so much. Thank you to Joe and Lavonne Plouff for letting us crash at your gorgeous space and get the bulk of these edits done!

Thank you to my Patreon supporters, clients, those who interview me, give me writing gigs, and help promote my work + my social media followers. You literally make this possible! A third whole book because of your support! This, like all of my books, is about what WE made. Thank you is an understatement, truly. You are so magical and wonderful.

To Chelsea, Drew, Zach, my Dad, and Ola: You already know how much I love and appreciate you (I hope) but here is yet another love note, yet another thank you note from me to you. I am such a proud Snow and so proud to be related to you all. So much thanks too to my Aunt Linda, Uncle Jim, and cousins Bradley, Kevin, and Hope for their ongoing support and unconditional love.

BethAnne, Troy, the kiddo, Jake, Kenny, Andrew, Libbie, Mickaylee, Kimby, my DnD groups, my Gadfly family, and the friends I've met online (and anyone important that I forgot! I'm sorry!): I could say something serious and profound here or I could thank you for the laughs. All of it is important—chosen family is tough but so are we. Love you all and am so grateful for you every day. To Theresa Reed and Melissa Cynova: thank you for always showing me who I want to be when I grow up and pushing me to grow that way.

Then there's Manny. How do you thank someone for literally everything without derailing your entire book? I'll figure it out one day; in the meantime, thanks specifically for letting me call the cat "thickeroni and cheese" incessantly. See you in like five seconds, probably.

About the Authors

Cassandra Snow is the two-time Weiser author of *Queering the Tarot* and *Queering Your Craft: Witchcraft from the Margins*. Professionally, Cassandra is a tarot reader and teacher who has taught students how to read cards in their own unique, personalized way everywhere from college campuses to burlesque studios. In their other life, Cassandra makes theatre happen, dabbles in storytelling and obsesses over tabletop roleplaying games, going hiking, and devouring books and movies. You can find out more about them at *www.cassandra-snow.com* or follow them in Instagram at *mx.cassandra.snow*.

Siri Vincent Plouff is a Nordic witch, writer, and teacher. They are a professional rune and tarot reader, and are the host of the *Heathen's Journey Podcast*. Their podcast is dedicated to creating space to learn about heathenry from an antiracist, queer perspective. Siri also teaches a wide variety of classes frequently—from classes about witchcraft to classes on runes. Their two signature courses are the Witchcraft Immersion and Radical Runes. For more information about these and other classes, please visit Siri's website at *www.northernlightswitch.com*. In their free time, Siri devours fiction, hangs out with their cats and spouse, and obsessively listens to podcasts.

To Our Readers

Weiser Books, an imprint of Red Wheel/Weiser, publishes books across the entire spectrum of occult, esoteric, speculative, and New Age subjects. Our mission is to publish quality books that will make a difference in people's lives without advocating any one particular path or field of study. We value the integrity, originality, and depth of knowledge of our authors.

Our readers are our most important resource, and we appreciate your input, suggestions, and ideas about what you would like to see published.

Visit our website at *www.redwheelweiser.com,* where you can learn about our upcoming books and free downloads, and also find links to sign up for our newsletter and exclusive offers.

You can also contact us at info@rwwbooks.com or at

Red Wheel/Weiser, LLC
65 Parker Street, Suite 7
Newburyport, MA 01950